D1405999

Virginie Fowler

PAPERWORKS

Colorful Crafts from Picture Eggs to Fish Kites

illustrations by the author

Prentice-Hall, Inc. / Englewood Cliffs, N.J.

PROPERTY OF
FAUQUIER COUNTY PUBLIC LIBRARY

For David Jeffrey Rothwell
a second book

Copyright © 1982 by Virginie Fowler Elbert
All rights reserved. No part of this book
may be reproduced in any form, or by any
means, except for the inclusion of brief
quotations in a review, without permission
in writing from the publisher.
Printed in the United States of America   · J

Prentice-Hall International, Inc., London
Prentice-Hall of Australia, Pty. Ltd., Sydney
Prentice-Hall Canada, Inc., Toronto
Prentice-Hall of India Private Ltd., New Delhi
Prentice-Hall of Japan, Inc., Tokyo
Prentice-Hall of Southeast Asia Pte. Ltd., Singapore
Whitehall Books Limited, Wellington, New Zealand
10 9 8 7 6 5 4 3

Library of Congress Cataloging in Publication Data
Elbert, Virginie.
    Paperworks: colorful crafts from picture eggs
to fish kites.
    Includes index.
    Summary: Presents a variety of projects including
jewelry, toys, and holiday decorations, made from
paper using such techniques as collage, papier mache,
printing, and various types of cutting and construction. Includes step-by-step illustrated instructions.
    1.   Paper work—Juvenile literature.
[1.   Paper work.   2.   Handicraft]   I.   Title.
TT870.E44 1982   745.54   82-9049
ISBN 0-13-648543-X
ISBN 0-13-648551-0 (pbk.)

745.54
Fow

Contents

Paper Crafts

Paper is the easiest craft material to use. In its many forms, it is easily available in art shops, craft shops, and stationery or card stores.

The use of paper for crafts goes back to ancient times; many of the same techniques are still used and the same objects are still being made in many countries. Among these are Japanese lanterns and paper kites; oriental screens; French and Asian papier-mâché boxes, jewelry, and art objects; middle European Christmas tree ornaments and toys; hand-printed papers in many techniques for covering decorative and useful objects.

Paper has been used as a means of communication from ancient Egyptian papyrus scrolls and Chinese rice paper scrolls, which told a story in pictures as the reader unrolled the length of paper, to modern mechanically printed books on rag or wood pulp paper. All these papers are made from products available in each country, and artists and craftspeople have long adapted these papers to their own uses. Not only did they use paper for drawings and paintings, but they decorated furniture with cut-out pictures, calling this technique decoupage and collage; they made boxes and even furniture with torn-up paper and glue, known as papier-mâché. In England in the middle of the nineteenth century, flat books of cut-out stage sets and characters were sold, known as "penny plain" and "tuppence colored." And who has not received lace-paper valentines and greeting cards at holidays and birthdays? Paper dolls have always been dressed in the clothes of the period, and some early ones are now collector's items. You will find descriptions of how to make many of these crafts in this book.

Here is a list of the papers and paper boards which are used in the craft designs in this book.

Types of Paper

Typewriter paper: plain white paper 8½ × 11 inches, used in this book mainly for pattern-making.

Onionskin paper: used for carbon copies of typed letters; thinner than typewriter paper but the same size.

Tissue paper: sold in folded packs as gift-wrapping, it is thicker or the same weight as onionskin, but thinner than typewriter paper. It is made in white, solid colors, and soft-colored stripes.

Tracing paper: see-through paper, stiffer than onionskin and less opaque; usually sold in pads of various sizes.

Drawing paper: thicker paper with a slightly rough surface on which you can use ink, poster paint, or acrylic paint. It is sold in pads or separate sheets in various sizes.

Construction paper: stiff paper in assorted colors, sold in pads or packs in various sizes.

Rice paper: thin but sturdy white paper, made in several thicknesses and surfaces and sold as separate sheets in various sizes.

Gift-wrap paper: sold in rolls or folded sheets in many colors and designs.

Wallpaper: stiff paper in solid colors or patterns. Samples can often be bought at home supply stores.

Shelf paper: sold in rolls 12 to 18 inches wide in solid colors or printed designs. Some types have a self-stick backing.

Con-Tact paper: self-stick paper in solid colors and designs, 18 inches wide, sold by the yard or half yard.

Types of Paper Board

All boards are sold in several sizes as separate sheets.

Bristol board: lightweight board with a smooth high gloss or dull white surface on both sides of the sheet.

Illustration board: heavier than bristol board, and sold in more than one thickness. The dull, slightly uneven surface is white on one side and has manufacturer's symbols on the other.

Poster board: approximately the weight of illustration board, with a dull flat surface in white or colors.

Mat board: stiff board in white, gold, silver, or colors.

Cardboard: comes in several thicknesses, usually with an unfinished tan or gray surface.

Corrugated cardboard: comes in various thicknesses, with tan color corrugations sandwiched between two thin cardboard surfaces.

Cardboard tubes: mailing tubes, paper towel, or bathroom tissue tubes made of lightweight, unfinished cardboard, usually gray in color.

Carefully read the next chapter for a description of processes which you will use over and over in paper craft designs. Each following chapter begins with a description of special processes used for that chapter's projects. So try your hand at the projects in this book, imagining that you are a craftsperson in another slot of time and in another country.

Some projects are easy to make; others are a little harder. In the Table of Contents, look for the projects marked "easy."

Before You Begin

Craft processes that are used throughout this book are described in this chapter, and you will be referred back to these pages.

In the beginning of the chapter "Cut and Glue," there are full descriptions of the techniques of *cutting* all types of paper and paper board, as well as techniques of *gluing*. So refer to pages 41 to 44 for both of these processes.

Enlarging and Reducing Designs

The patterns for each project are drawn to scale on a grid. The enlarging information is printed just below the lower right-hand corner of the grid. Increase the size of the grid squares to the measurement shown—½ inch, ¾ inch, or 1 inch.

On typewriter paper or graph paper, measure and draw larger squares, matching the enlarging information. Number the lines. If the enlarged drawing is larger than a sheet of typewriter paper, tape several sheets together to make one large sheet. You can also use ¼-inch-squared graph paper. Count off the number of squares needed for the enlargement, and with a ruler and pencil draw the vertical and horizontal lines. For instance, for an enlargement to 1-inch squares, count off four ¼-inch squares and make a heavy pencil line. Number the lines.

Now all you have to do is draw in the lines of the pattern drawing on the larger squares, following the lines on the smaller grid. Draw across each square in the same place and cut across each grid line at the same place. When you are finished, you will have an exact enlargement of the original pattern.

To reduce a drawing, make the final grid on the typewriter paper smaller than the original pattern grid.

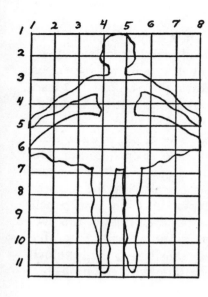

Pattern

Enlarge to ⅜" squares

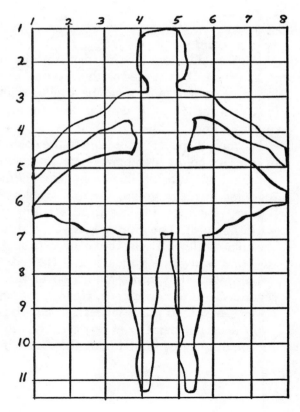

Enlarged Drawing

Lead-Pencil Transfer Paper

Once the enlarged pattern is made, it is easy to transfer it to the final paper or paper board with lead-pencil transfer paper.

Make the paper by covering a sheet of typewriter paper, or other lightweight paper, with criss-crossing strokes of a *soft* lead pencil until the surface is as dark as you can make it without digging into the paper.

To transfer a pattern, hold the final sheet of paper flat on the working surface, using small pieces of tape at each corner. On top of it place the enlarged pattern drawing and hold it in place with small pieces of tape at each upper corner. Slip the transfer paper between these two sheets of paper, with the lead pencil side against the bottom sheet. Draw around all lines of the pattern with a *hard* lead pencil. Lift the pattern and the transfer paper to make sure all lines have been transferred; then remove the pattern and transfer paper and continue with the project.

Painting

Acrylic Paint

The best all-around paint for the projects in this book is acrylic paint. It can be thinned with water or acrylic polymer medium for a transparent look; it can be applied thickly so as to be opaque; it is waterproof, so it can be used on all projects, and it dries quickly.

Buy acrylic paint in tubes. Use the color directly from the tube or mix two colors together to form another color. For instance, if you have one tube of blue and one of yellow, mix equal amounts together to make green. Or mix a color with white to form a lighter, opaque color. To form a transparent color, mix water with the paint. The more water you add, the thinner and lighter the color will be. Always have an extra sheet of the same paper as the final project on which to test the paint.

Before starting to mix paint, cover the working surface with several sheets of newspaper. Have extra papers handy so you can cover any spilled paint with fresh paper.

Since acrylic paint dries very quickly, use throwaway containers for mixing pans: individual aluminum foil cupcake pans are good, or small plastic drinking cups. After putting on the first coat of paint, let it dry before adding the second coat. To keep a special mixed color from drying out, put the paint in a small jar with a tight-fitting cover. This way, the paint will be liquid for the second coat.

There are two *acrylic polymer mediums* that can be used with acrylic paints. One is *gloss* which is added to the paint as a thin= ner, instead of water, to give the paint a high gloss when dry The other is *matte*, which lessens the shine of the paint. Both can be used as a final coat over a painted surface. The gloss can also be used as a glue for collage or decoupage work.

Always wipe off the screw top and the cap of a paint tube right after using it. Otherwise the cap will stick and be hard to take off the tube the next time you use the paint. Do the same for the jars of gloss or matte medium. And always squeeze tubes from the bottom.

When you use acrylic paint, you will need soft nylon brushes, either flat or round, as they do not leave brush marks on the paint. The exception is a stencil brush, which is round with a flat bottom and is made from stiff bristles. Always keep a jar of clean water beside you when you work. Keep the brushes in the water when you are not using them so paint will not harden on the bristles. Wipe off the water with a cloth, facial tissues, or paper towels before dipping the brush in the color. When you are through, wash the brush thoroughly with soap and water. If any paint does dry on a brush, use denatured alcohol to remove it.

Poster Paint

Poster paint can be used instead of acrylic paint, but it is not as permanent. It has a chalky surface, and if applied too thickly it will flake off when dry. It can be thinned with water, but it will always be opaque, never completely transparent. For some of the projects, poster paint will work best, so follow paint suggestions in each project.

Poster paint is sold in jars and also in tubes marked *gouache,* which is the French name for an opaque watercolor paint.

Use soft watercolor brushes, not nylon brushes, when painting with poster paint or gouache.

Enamel Paint and Shellac

Before covering a cardboard or wood object with enamel paint, "seal" all the surfaces with one or two coats of shellac. Apply shellac with a flat watercolor brush; after using, clean the brush with denatured alcohol.

When the shellac is dry, open the can of enamel paint and stir the contents slowly and carefully with a thin stick until the surface is an even color. Flow paint on the shellacked surface with a flat watercolor brush, trying not to go over the same area too many times. After the first coat has dried, add a second coat. Let the paint dry for at least 24 hours before handling the enameled surface.

Warning: If the shellac coat or the first coat of enamel has a rough surface when dry, smooth it out with sandpaper before adding a second coat.

Mobile Forms

Wire Coat Hangers

Make a mobile form from two wire coat hangers. Cut off the bottom half of each hanger with a wire clipper. Pull up the top wires until they form a straight line rather than a sloping one.

Slowly turn the hook of one hanger so that it is at right angles to the top wire of the hanger. Do this very slowly, as a quick turn may snap off the hook. Bind the hooks of the two hangers together with black masking tape.

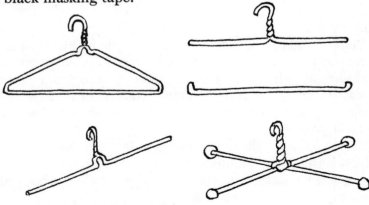

Wire Coat Hanger Mobile

Push a fishing-float cork or bottle cork over each cut end of wire. The corks can be painted with black or colored acrylic paint. Hang the mobile objects with string or heavy thread from the four lengths of wire. If the string or thread slips on the wire, hold it in place with a small piece of tape.

Cardboard Circle

Cut a circle from heavy cardboard; the size depends on the number and size of the objects to be hung from the mobile form. With a thin nail, skewer, or large needle, punch holes ½ to ¾ inch in from the edge of the cardboard circle. Make the same number of holes as the objects to be hung.

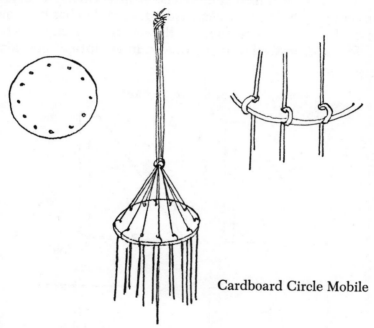

Cardboard Circle Mobile

For each hole, cut one long piece of string or heavy thread. The strings hold the separate objects below the circle; make each one hang at a different height. Each string goes through its hole and is tied to hold it in place. Then all the strings are tied together 6 to 8 inches above the circle. Finally, the group of strings is knotted near the top; this final knot will slip over whatever hook is the final hanging place. See diagrams for all these steps.

Cardboard Supports

To display a picture frame on a table, or a character or furniture on a stage, make a triangle support. Medium-weight cardboard is the best material to use. Measure and cut the cardboard with a craft knife into a triangular shape with a flap on the straight side. The height should be a little shorter than the object to be supported and the base wide enough to support the object. Make the flap ¼ to 1 inch wide, depending on the size of the triangle and the object to be supported.

Score the long edge of the flap where it joins the triangle and bend at a right angle to the triangle. Trim off part of the bottom of the triangle, starting at the base of the flap line and angling up to the outer edge ⅜ inch or more above the bottom (see diagram). This cut may have to be deepened after the flap has been pasted down. If it is not deep enough, the object to be supported will fall forward, instead of being braced in an upright position.

Cardboard Support

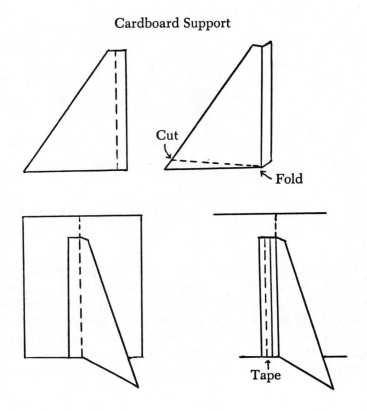

Measure and draw a vertical line down the middle of the back of the object to be supported. Brush glue on the outside of the flap and place the scored edge along the center pencil line. Flatten out the triangle support and place a heavy book over the flap until the glue dries.

If the support is a large one and the object to be supported is very heavy, strengthen the flap with a line of tape, half on the flap and half on the object. You can also strengthen the opposite side of the support in the same way with tape, half on the back of the triangle and half on the object.

Helpful Hints

Keep a bowl of water, a sponge, and paper towels beside you to quickly clean up your hands or work surface. Also have a box of facial tissues nearby for blotting up extra white glue or smoothing down just-glued paper or wiping a paint brush.

Put a layer of newspapers over the working surface; add another layer when the paper gets paint-spattered or sticky with glue.

Always have a roll of self-sticking tape or masking tape handy to quickly hold a project in place.

Ask an older person for permission to use sharp knives or other tools, to use kitchen or household equipment, to put a nail in a wall for a picture, or to hang a mobile from a light fixture.

You may need an older person to help in cutting some types of cardboard or illustration board with a craft knife, or to help find a place where a project can stay undisturbed for several hours.

And, like all craftspeople, wear a smock or apron when you are working.

Printed Paper

Techniques of Printed Paper Crafts

Printed paper is used to decorate all the crafts in this chapter and some in other chapters. Instead of using commercially printed paper, you can make your own for all those projects that list printed paper. There are many craft ways of printing paper in overall repeated patterns, such as rubbings, styrofoam blocks, cellulose sponge or vegetables, roll-on designs, stencils, or marbleizing. For all these methods, the colors are either acrylic paints or water-base block printing inks printed on plain white or colored papers.

All the printing techniques are explained in this chapter, and many of the designs in the projects can be adapted to other printing techniques.

RUBBINGS

You can copy any raised design by putting a sheet of paper over the object, then rubbing a pencil back and forth over the surface. Look around the house or neighborhood for metal, wood, or stone objects with raised designs. You'll find coins, handles of forks and spoons, straw baskets or place mats, caned chair seats, pierced metal radiator covers, carved wooden box covers, cut glass dishes, a scallop shell, a fossil fish or leaf, stone ornaments on buildings or designs on old gravestones, and many, many other objects.

Materials and Tools

thin paper: onionskin, tissue paper, tracing paper, or rice paper
pencil: soft lead pencil, carpenter's pencil, china marker pencil,
    colored pencils, or crayons

scissors
ruler
masking tape
rubber cement (optional)

Making the Rubbing

Cut a piece of paper a little larger than the object to be copied. For small objects such as coins, use a folded piece of masking tape or rubber cement under each one to hold it in place on the working surface. Tape the paper over the object.

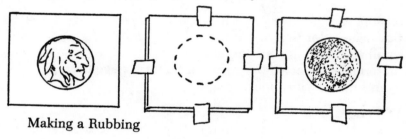

Making a Rubbing

Rub the pencil very lightly over the paper, just above the object. Gradually increase the pressure to bring out the design. A coin should result in a dark design against a lighter background. You may have to make several tries before you are satisfied. Just work slowly and very carefully.

A SHELL PICTURE

Make color rubbings of several scallop shells on one sheet of paper, then mount the sheet behind a mat and display the picture on a table or shelf. It is fun to make this picture in the winter, just to remind you of summertime. Or you can pick any other small object to make your rubbing picture.

Materials and Tools
thin paper, white or a pale color
pencil crayons, any color
1 or more scallop shells
white household glue
masking tape
pencil
ruler
scissors
flat watercolor brush, 1 inch wide
small container for mixing glue
materials and tools for matting a picture, page 66,
    and making a support, page 10

Directions
    1. Make rubbings of several scallop shells on one sheet of paper, or repeat the rubbing of one shell. You can use one colored pencil for all the shells, or make each shell a different color. Follow the directions for making rubbings in the beginning of this chapter.
    2. Make a mat for the shell picture, following directions on page 66. The mat can be a plain color that matches or contrasts with the color of the shells.

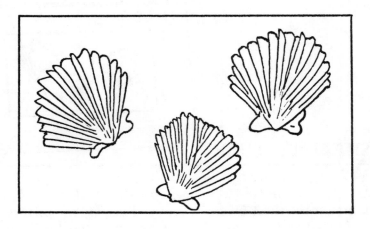

Step 1

3. Back the picture and mat with a sheet of illustration board, adding an easel-type support at the back.

STYROFOAM BLOCK PRINTING

Styrofoam block printing designs can be cut and printed as flat solid-color designs or outline designs to be printed on colored paper. The raised design can be used over and over; it can be printed in more than one color and at any angle. Use styrofoam sheet bought at any art store, or a piece of packing material.

Materials and Tools
styrofoam sheet, 1¼ inches thick,
   and as large as needed
typewriter paper
clear plastic wrap, 6 inches square
ball of absorbent cotton, 1¼ inches in diameter
string
tubes of acrylic paint or water-base
   block printing ink
masking tape
pencil
ruler
scissors
craft knife
flat plastic coffee can cover
plastic spoon
lots of newspapers

Cutting Out the Styrofoam Block
Make a pattern for your design on the typewriter paper and cut it out. Lay the paper pattern on the block's top surface and trace around the edges of the design with a lead pencil. With the craft knife, cut into the styrofoam along the pencil line to a depth of ¼ inch. Then cut away the rest of the styrofoam around the outside of the design to a depth of ¼ inch. The design will then be higher than the background.

Making a Paint Dabber
Paint is transferred to the styrofoam block design with a dabber. To make the dabber, lightly roll a piece of absorbent cotton

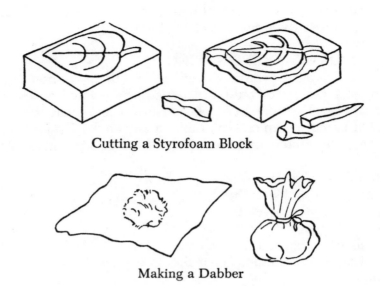

Cutting a Styrofoam Block

Making a Dabber

into a ball, 1¼ inches in diameter. Put the ball in the middle of a 6-inch square piece of clear plastic wrap. Bring the sides of the wrap up around the cotton and tie with string close to the top of the cotton ball. Pound the dabber lightly against a flat surface to flatten the bottom.

Mixing Paint

You have a choice of paints for printing, depending on which kind is easiest for you to buy. One is acrylic paint and the other is water-base block printing ink. Both are sold in tubes and come in a number of colors.

First spread newspaper over the working surface. Squeeze out about 2 inches of paint or ink in the center of a plastic coffee can cover. Mix in a little water, stirring with a plastic spoon. The paint or ink should be quite thick.

Dip the dabber into the paint with a quick up-and-down motion; then transfer the paint to the styrofoam design with the same dabbing motion. Turn over the styrofoam block and press the raised design against a test sheet of paper. Repeat two or three times. If the paint is too thin, add more paint; if too thick, add more water and test again.

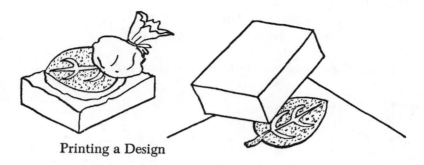

Printing a Design

Proceed with the final printing, mixing more paint as needed. Put the printed paper on a flat surface to dry overnight.

FANCY LOOSE-LEAF FOLDERS

Decorate a loose-leaf binder to hold your school papers, or as a gift recipe holder for a cook. You can also make your own folder covers from heavy corrugated cardboard and loose-leaf rings. Either kind is covered outside and inside with printed paper.

Materials and Tools
hardcover loose-leaf binder, 9¾ × 11½ × 1¾ inches,
   or 2 sheets of heavy corrugated cardboard, 9¾ × 11½, and
   3 loose-leaf snap rings, 1¾ inches in diameter

solid color paper for label
4 sheets of printed paper, see sizes in Step 1
self-sticking solid color tape, 1½ inches wide
white household glue
package of white paper with pre-punched holes
pencil
ruler
scissors
craft knife
flat watercolor brush, 1 inch wide
small container for mixing glue
black felt-tipped pen
materials and tools for cutting and printing styrofoam block

Directions

1. Choose a design that fits your project and cut it from a styrofoam block. See suggested designs or adapt any other designs in this chapter. Print four sheets of paper, 9¾ × 11½ inches, following directions at the beginning of the chapter.

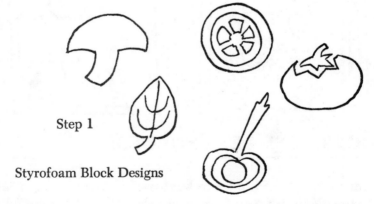

Step 1

Styrofoam Block Designs

2. For the loose-leaf folder of heavy corrugated cardboard, measure two pieces, 9¾ × 11½, and cut with the craft knife.

3. To cover either the binder or the corrugated cardboard with the printed paper, first mix white glue with a little water in the small container. Apply glue with the flat brush to the front of one piece of cardboard or the front of the binder. Lay one sheet of printed paper over the glue and smooth into place. Repeat on

opposite side of cardboard or binder cover. Repeat on other piece of cardboard or the back cover of the binder. Put several heavy books over the glued paper until glue is dry.

4. Measure and cut tape into four 9¾-inch lengths and into four 11½-inch lengths. If you are covering a binder, you will need two extra pieces of tape 1¾ inches long for the top and bottom of the spine.

5. Cover the edges of the cardboard with the tape, starting with the 11½-inch sides, allowing ¾ inch on each side of the edge. Repeat with the 9¾-inch sides. For the binder, cover edges in the same way, and also cover the top and bottom of the spine. You may have to cut away excess tape on the inside of the top and bottom.

6. Place a sheet of paper with pre-punched holes over the outside of one piece of covered cardboard. With a pencil, mark the position of the two or three holes. Punch out holes with either a hand punch or nail. Repeat on the other piece of covered cardboard. Put the pack of pre-punched paper between the two pieces of covered cardboard and insert the snap rings. Or fill binder with paper.

7. Cut a label from the plain paper and glue it on the front of the folder or binder.

Variation With Covered Spine

Variation: Cut the printed paper for the binder ½ inch wider on all four sides. Turn this margin over to the inside on three sides and glue in place. Glue the margin on the fourth side over the spine area. Repeat on back of binder. Cut a strip of paper to cover the spine and glue it in place. Line the inside of the front and back of the binder with plain color paper.

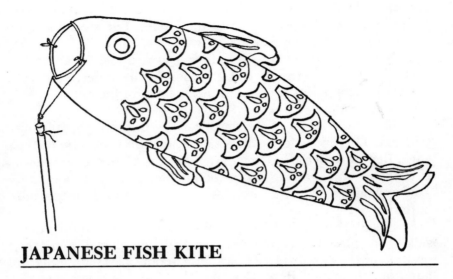

JAPANESE FISH KITE

On Boy's Day in Japan, two-sided paper fish kites fly on long thin poles outside each house where a boy lives. The paper is white with a brightly printed design, and the fishes are made in many sizes and colors. This one is 24 inches long, but you can make any size by changing the measurements of the fish design and the size of the printed fish scale.

Materials and Tools
lightweight white drawing paper or lightweight
   rice paper, 21 × 31 inches
typewriter paper
wooden dowel, ¼ × ¼ × 36 inches
white self-sticking tape, ½ inch wide
tubes of acrylic paint or water-base block
   printing ink, red and yellow
thin wire, 12 inches
thin cord or string, 2 yards
white household glue
pencil
ruler
scissors
black felt-tipped pen

flat watercolor brush, 1 inch wide
round nylon brush, #5
materials and tools for cutting and painting
    1½-inch thick styrofoam block
facial tissues

Directions

1. Glue or tape together several sheets of typewriter paper to make a sheet for the fish pattern.

2. Enlarge the fish pattern on the typewriter paper by the grid method. Also enlarge the scale and fin patterns by the grid method on separate sheets of typewriter paper. Cut out all patterns.

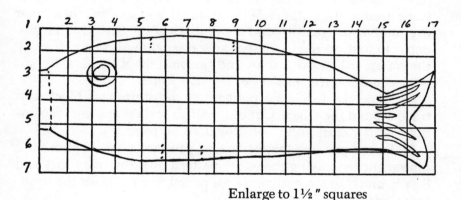

Enlarge to 1½" squares

Upper Fin   Lower Fin   Scale

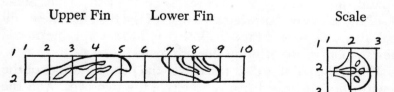

Enlarge to 1½" squares

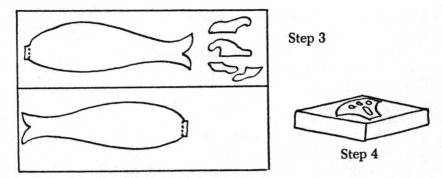

Step 3

Step 4

3. Trace around the outline of the fish on one half of the kite paper. Turn the fish over and trace around the outline on the other half of the kite paper. At the other end of the kite paper, trace around the outlines of the top and bottom fins; turn them over and again trace around the outlines of the fins. Cut the kite paper in half, so the two fishes are on separate sheets. Cut away the fin area. You can cut around the outlines of the fins, but *do not cut around the outlines of the two fishes.*

4. Place the fish scale pattern on the styrofoam block and trace around the edges. Cut out the fish scale shape and decorations with a craft knife (see directions on page 15).

5. Before printing the fish scales, you may want to plan their placement by moving the paper pattern over the two fishes and lightly marking the outline with a pencil as a guide for the styrofoam printing block.

6. Follow directions on pages 15–17 for making dabber, mixing paint, and printing the fish scales on the fish shape. Some parts of the scales will overlap the edges of the fish, but these will be cut away. Be sure to tape the kite paper to several thicknesses of newspaper before printing the fish scales.

7. When the paint is dry, trace over the pencil outlines of the fish with the felt-tipped pen; also circle the two eyes. Add the black lines on the fins and tail. Fill in the center marks on each fish scale with yellow paint, using the round #5 brush.

8. Cut out the two fish shapes, just outside the black outlines. Turn one fish over and with the flat brush spread a ½-inch wide strip of thinned white glue all around the edge, *except the mouth and the end of the tail.* Carefully lay the other fish, right side up,

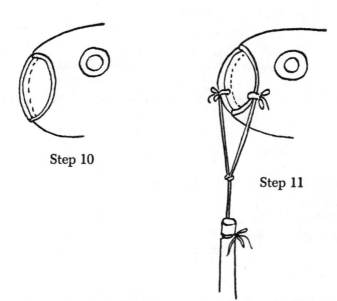

Step 10

Step 11

over the first one. Press all around the edges with a wadded piece of facial tissue. Let dry.

9. Glue the two upper fins opposite each other on each side of the fish. Repeat with lower fins.

10. Curve the wire into an oval that fits the mouth opening, cutting away any extra wire. Hold the wire in place by folding over the paper margin around the mouth and gluing it in position. When glue is dry, strengthen the edge with self-sticking tape.

11. Notch the dowel, ½ inch from one end. Tie the middle of the cord around the notch. Bring the two lengths of cord together and knot them together, 10 inches from the two free ends. Make a small hole at each side of the mouth opening and pass each cord through a hole, tying the end around the wire.

12. Hold the dowel straight up over your head and run—the air will rush through the fish and it will swell out. You can also attach the fish to a longer pole stuck in the ground where it will catch the breeze, or hang it by mouth and tail from a center light fixture so the wind from a window will make it swing around.

Variation: Fish scales can be a solid color without the cutout yellow decorations.

CELLULOSE SPONGE PRINTING

A cellulose sponge (kitchen sponge) with its irregular surface openings creates interesting printed designs on paper. The sponge can be used full size to print an overall oblong design, or cut into small shapes—square, round, diamond, or whatever. The printing technique is the same as styrofoam block printing, except that you do not need a dabber.

Materials and Tools

unused cellulose sponge
tubes of acrylic paint or water-base
    block printing ink
black felt-tipped pen
typewriter paper
pencil
ruler
scissors
aluminum-foil pie plate or
    plastic coffee can cover
plastic spoon
lots of newspaper

Preparing the Sponge for Printing

Run water over the sponge and then squeeze out as much water as you can. Let the sponge dry until it is just slightly damp.

If you are going to cut the sponge into smaller shapes, measure and draw a pattern on the typewriter paper. Cut out the pattern. Placing it on the sponge, trace around the pattern edges with the felt-tipped pen. Cut around the pen line with the scissors.

Cellulose Sponge Printing

Printing With the Sponge

Spread newspapers over the working surface. If you are using a full-size sponge, you will need an aluminum-foil pie plate for mixing the paint or ink; for a smaller piece of sponge, use a plastic coffee can cover. Follow the directions in Styrofoam Block Printing (page 16) for mixing acrylic paint or water-base block printing ink. The mixture can be a little thinner for sponge printing.

Lightly press the slightly damp, flat surface of the sponge on the ink, then press it on the paper. Continue until the design is complete. Let the printed paper dry overnight on a flat surface.

Variation: Vegetables and fruits, such as mushrooms, beets, radishes, oranges, or lemons, can be cut in half and their flat cut surfaces pressed into paint or ink and then against paper.

SPECIAL GIFT CARDS

Everyone likes to receive a greeting card: at holidays, tucked into a gift box as a surprise from a friend, or for a birthday. If you cut a cellulose sponge design, you can make several cards from the one design. This is very handy, especially at holidays or for birthdays.

Materials and Tools
drawing paper, white or colored in any size
typewriter paper
tube or tubes of acrylic paint
pencil
ruler
scissors
materials and tools for cutting and printing
  with cellulose sponge

Directions
   1. You can print your gift card as a single sheet of paper, fold the paper in half, or fold it in fours. Whichever way, enlarge the design to fit the front surface of the paper.

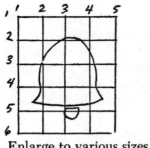

Enlarge to various sizes

Flower Design

Bell Design

2. Choose one of the designs and enlarge it by the grid method on the typewriter paper. You can also make your own design.

3. Cut the cellulose sponge, following directions on page 24.

4. Put newspapers over the working surface. Mix the paint and print the design, following directions on page 24. Lay all cards flat until dry. Then write a message inside each card.

ROLL-ON PRINTING

Roll-on printing forms a continuous design over paper. The design surface is made of thick, absorbent soft string pressed into a rubber-cement-covered cardboard tube. The string is inked by rolling it over paint or ink; then the inked string is rolled over the paper. Repeat the inking and rolling until the paper is covered. One design can be criss-crossed with the same design in the same color, or a similar design in another color.

Materials and Tools
cardboard mailing tube, paper towel tube,
   or bathroom tissue tube
paper for printing
thick soft string
rubber cement, 4-ounce jar
wooden dowel, ⅜ to ½ inch in diameter,
   6 inches longer than cardboard tube
tubes of acrylic paint or water-base block printing ink
pencil
scissors
ruler

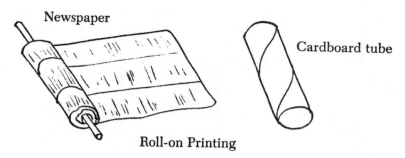

Newspaper

Cardboard tube

Roll-on Printing

shallow rectangular container for paint, slightly
   wider than the tube
lots of newspapers

Preparing the Roller

Make your first roller no longer than 4½ to 6 inches. Once you
have made your first roller, you can move on to larger ones.

Measure and cut a full length of a section of newspaper, making it ½ inch less in width than the cardboard tube. Cut a
wooden dowel 6 inches longer than the tube. Center the dowel at
one narrow end of the length of newspaper and tightly roll the
paper around the dowel until the roll is slightly smaller in diameter than the tube.

Push the rolled paper and dowel into the cardboard tube. The
ends of the rolled paper will be just inside the edges of the tube.
Three inches of the wooden dowel handles will stick out at each
end of the tube.

Holding the tube by one of the dowel handles, cover the cardboard surface with rubber cement. Let dry and brush on a second
coat.

Starting at one edge of the tube, add a fresh strip of rubber
cement and press string into it to form a pattern. Keep adding
rubber cement and string until you cover the cardboard tube.
Let the cement dry well before using the roller.

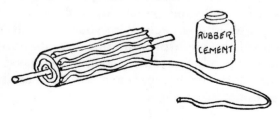

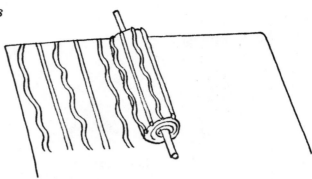

Printing With the Roller

Squeeze acrylic paint or water-base block printing ink in the center of the shallow pan and mix with water. Roll the patterned tube over the pan, allowing the string to soak up the paint or ink. Holding the roller by the dowel handles, run it over the paper. Do not let the ink thin out too much; replace the color as often as needed to keep a fairly even tone. When the paper has been covered with the printed design, let it dry overnight on a flat surface.

You can make more than one roller design, printing each one in a different color. The colors may overlap in some areas, so make sure that each color is dry before adding another color to the paper.

GIFT WRAP PAPER

Decorate plain colored shelf paper, large sheets of thin white paper, or brown wrapping paper with your own roll-on designs (or use any one of the other printing processes described in this chapter). Make as much or as little paper as you need. You can fold small pieces of the printed paper to use as gift cards, writing your message inside.

Materials and Tools

plain colored shelf paper, thin white paper,
    or brown wrapping paper
tubes of acrylic paint, any color
newspapers
materials and tools for printing roll-on designs

Directions

1. Spread newspapers over working and drying surfaces.

2. Prepare the roll-on printing design, following directions on page 27.

3. Spread out the paper to be printed; print it; and let it dry.

4. Make matching gift cards by folding pieces of printed paper in half.

5. Wrap your gifts and tie with matching or contrasting colored ribbon, then attach the gift cards.

STENCILING

Stencil paper is a thin but stiff waterproof paper. Stencils are made by cutting out a design in the stencil paper, then dabbing acrylic paint with a special brush through the cutout openings onto the paper to be printed. For a design of several colors, cut separate stencils, one for each color.

Materials and Tools

stencil paper
typewriter paper
lightweight cardboard, 1 inch larger
    than the typewriter paper
paper for printing
pencil
ruler
black felt-tipped pen
masking tape
craft knife
tubes of acrylic paint
round stencil brush, ¾ inch in diameter
plastic coffee can top or aluminum-foil pie plate
lots of newspapers
paper towels
clear plastic wrap

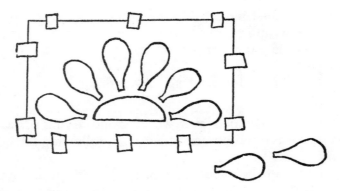

Cutting a Stencil

Make a pencil drawing of a stencil design on typewriter paper. This can be either a freehand design or one enlarged by the grid method. Trace over the pencil lines with the black felt-tipped pen. Tape the drawing to the cardboard with masking tape.

Cut a piece of stencil paper an inch wider than the outlines of the drawing. Place over the design, taping the edges with masking tape.

Holding the knife like a pencil, bring it toward you as you cut into the stencil paper. Follow the black outlines of the design beneath. When all the areas of the design have been cut away, remove the stencil paper from the cardboard. Tape it to whatever surface is to be decorated.

Tip: If you are making your own design, be sure that all openings are separated by paper "lines" which are attached to each other (see diagram).

Stencil paper

Printing a Stencil Design

Squeeze a small ribbon of acrylic paint on a plastic coffee can top or a throwaway aluminum-foil pie plate. With an up-and-down movement, touch the bottom of the stencil brush to the paint; lightly dab the brush on newspaper to get rid of excess paint and to spread the paint across the surface of the brush hairs. Holding the brush upright, dab the paint in the stencil design openings. When the design has been completely filled in, remove the tape and quickly lift the stencil paper *straight up* so as not to smear the edges of the design.

When printing a repeat design, the stencil paper may cover part of the first printed design, so let the paint dry thoroughly. However, if the stencil paper does not cover the design, continue printing, following directions in the previous paragraph. Also, if you are making a regular, repeated design, lightly square off the paper and print on any square, as you will not have to worry about overlapping of stencil paper.

Wash the brush in water and wipe dry with paper towels if you have to stop between printings. Also cover the paint dish with clear plastic wrap so the paint will not dry out. Add a little water if it does start to dry.

If you are printing a design that has two or more colors, cut a stencil for each color. If this is a repeat pattern, stencil one color throughout all the repeats and let the paint dry. Repeat printing with a second stencil and color, and with a third stencil and color if needed.

One color   Two colors   Three colors

You can also add separate colors to the different sections of one stencil. These colors, too, have to be added while the stencil is in position, so quickly wash out the brush for each color or have extra brushes handy.

SPLASHY SHOPPING BAGS

Decorate plain paper shopping bags with your own stenciled designs. Big splashy designs can be made from small stencil shapes repeated to form a larger design. Here are two simple shapes, **a** square and a triangle, that can form many designs.

Materials and Tools
plain paper shopping bag, 13 × 15½ inches
typewriter paper
stencil paper
tubes of acrylic paint, any colors
pencil
ruler
scissors
compass
newspapers
materials and tools for cutting and printing stencil

Directions for Sunburst Pattern
   1. Transfer the triangle pattern to a sheet of typewriter paper by the grid method. Cut out the stencil, following directions on page 30.
   2. With the compass, draw a circle, 5 inches in diameter, in the center of both sides of a plain shopping bag. If the bag has a border top or bottom or both, you will have to place your circle off-center, or make a smaller circle.

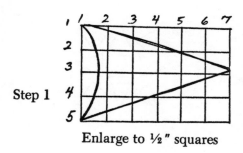

Step 1

Enlarge to ½″ squares

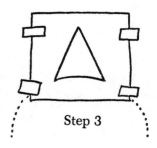

Step 3

3. Put a folded section of newspaper inside the bag to keep the paint from going through to the other side of the bag. Repeat the stencil pattern eight times around the edge of the circle. When the paint is dry, turn the bag to the other side and repeat the stencil pattern. Let paint dry.

Directions for Square Design

1. For the square design, measure and lightly draw a rectangle of 3 squares across and 5 squares down in the center of each side of the shopping bag. The size of the squares depends on the area of the bag you want to cover. For instance, for 2-inch squares, measure an area 6 × 10 inches.

2. Follow directions for cutting a stencil on page 30.

3. Put a folded section of newspaper inside the bag to protect it during stenciling. Put the stencil in position and paint the design, moving the stencil from square to square. Follow directions in the beginning of this chapter.

4. The whole design can be one color with the background of the paper showing in alternate squares; or you can use two or more colors for the design.

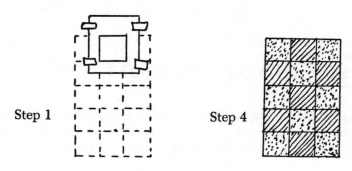

Step 1

Step 4

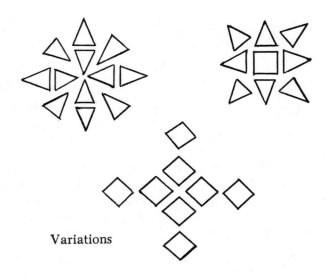

Variations

Variations: See diagrams for other designs using the triangle and square. The two designs can also be cut from a styrofoam block and printed as a block design.

ENTERTAINING STENCILED GIFTS

Here are stencil designs that can be used to decorate paper napkins, paper guest towels, and memo pads. You can use any color acrylic paint and any color paper items. Only one suggestion—

pick contrasting paint and paper colors. Yellow paint on a yellow background or pale blue against a pale blue background will hardly be seen. You can, though, choose dark blue paint for a pale blue background, or vice versa.

Materials and Tools
stencil paper
typewriter paper
paper napkins, paper guest towels, or memo pad
pencil
ruler
scissors
materials and tools for cutting and coloring stencil project

Directions
1. Pick a design and enlarge it by the grid method.
2. Cut out the stencil and print the design, following instructions for stenciling on page 30. Let paint dry well before using the paper.

Step 1

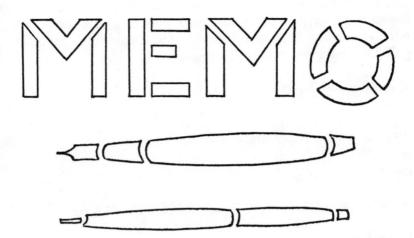

Special Instruction: Open up the napkins and paper towels and place them over newspapers so you have only one thickness. If they are left folded, the paint will sink into the other sections of the paper, and the napkins and towels will stick together. For the memo pads, cut newspaper into pieces the size of the pad. As you print each sheet of memo paper, turn it back and slip a piece of newspaper between the printed side and the previous sheet. You can lightly hold down the printed pages with a book (see drawing).

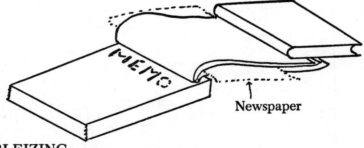

Newspaper

MARBLEIZING

You can make marbleized paper just like the endpapers of old books. Use it to cover boxes, writing folders, memo pads, or personal telephone books; you can also use it to make necklace beads. These projects are scattered throughout the book, so look in the index to locate them.

Materials and Tools

white drawing paper, 8 × 11 inches, as many as
    you plan to marbleize
tubes of oil paint: 1 or 2 bright colors plus brown,
    dark blue, or dark green
turpentine
small plastic throw-away drinking cups
cardboard, 8 × 10 inches
shallow throw-away aluminum-foil pan, approximately
    10 × 14 inches
plastic spoons
plastic fork or wooden stirrer
flat stiff oil paint brush
lots of newspapers

Preparing the Marbleized Design

Cover the working and drying areas with newspapers. Place
the aluminum-foil pan on the newspapers and add 1 inch of cold
water. Place the sheets of drawing paper to be printed to one side
of the aluminum-foil pan.

Mix oil paints separately in plastic throw-away drinking cups,
using plastic spoons. Add enough turpentine to thin the paint to a
liquid as thick as heavy cream. Lightly pour small gobs of paint
here and there on the water surface, so they float on the top.
Also, using the brush loaded with paint, shake small drops of
paint onto the water surface. Pull the paint lightly over the surface with the fork or stirrer, so the different colors form a pattern
but do not blend with each other. Or lean over one end of the
pan and blow gently at the surface to move the paint around in a
swirling design.

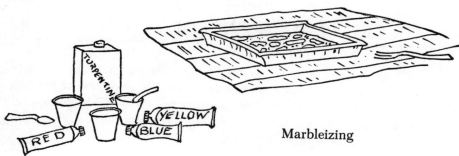

Marbleizing

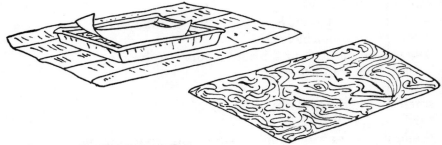

Printing the Design on Paper

When the surface of the water is covered with the marble design, quickly lay a sheet of paper over the paint, holding the paper at opposite corners, curved up slightly. The center of the sheet should touch the oiled water first; then quickly let down the ends. Tap the surface lightly to release air bubbles. Quickly lift the paper up and away from the paint surface, turn it over, and lay it flat on the drying area.

Repeat the printing with as many sheets of paper as you want, adding paint when needed and swirling it into new patterns. If the paint gets muddy, pull the edge of a piece of cardboard over the surface to clean it. Let the paper dry well before using it.

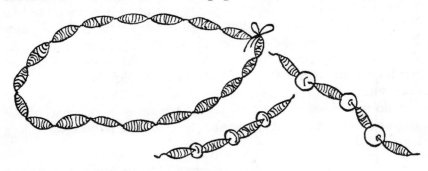

ROLLED BEAD NECKLACE

Roll up long triangles of marbleized paper to make narrow beads. Make the beads all the same length or different lengths and string them on heavy button or carpet thread. Mix plain and printed beads in one necklace; or add fat round beads of papier-mâché pulp (see page 108 for directions).

Materials and Tools
marbleized paper (follow directions for making paper)
construction paper, any color (optional)
white household glue
acrylic polymer gloss medium (optional)
button or carpet thread
pencil
ruler
scissors
thin nail, small metal skewer, or super-thin
    drinking straw
flat watercolor brush, 1 inch wide
round nylon brush, #5 (optional)
large-eyed needle
small container for mixing glue

Directions
1. Each bead is made from a long narrow triangle of printed
or plain colored paper, 1¼ inches wide at one end and 8½ inches
long; or use a narrower width and shorter length. You can
measure and cut out one triangle, then use it as a pattern, tracing
around the edges with a pencil. Make as many triangles as you
need for a necklace long enough to go over your head. You can fit
the same-size triangles close together on a sheet of paper, so that
as you are cutting out one triangle, you are cutting out part of the
next one (see diagram).

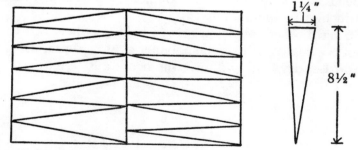

Step 1

1¼ "

8½ "

2. Mix white household glue in a small container with a little
water. Brush glue very thinly on the wrong side of the triangle,
except for the first ¾ inch at the broad end. Keep glue just inside
the long edges.

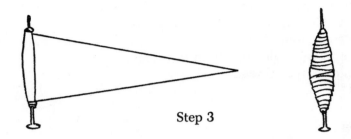

Step 3

3. With the triangle flat on the working surface, place the thin nail, skewer, or drinking straw across the edge of the broad end. Roll the paper around this center core. Continue to roll the core evenly toward the pointed end, tightening the paper as you go along. When the point is reached, smooth it into place and wipe off any excess glue. Slip the bead off the core and set it aside to dry. Repeat the process until all your beads are made.

4. When the beads are thoroughly dry, thread the needle with the button or carpet thread and string the beads. Knot the two ends of the thread and cut off the ends, leaving about ½ inch of thread at each end. Poke the free ends down into a bead on either side. Or just make a bow and let the ends hang free.

Variations: Cut ⅜-inch circles of stiff paper. Punch a hole in the center of each circle and string between the beads.

Beads can be rolled without glue, adding glue only on the last 1½ inch at the pointed end.

String finished beads on thread held taut between two jars. Paint the beads with acrylic polymer gloss medium, using the #5 brush. Let dry. This will give the beads a high gloss.

Cut and Glue

Techniques of Cutting Paper

Here are the basic directions for cutting all the kinds of paper, cardboard, and heavy art board you will be using in this chapter and all through the book. The tools you will need are very simple: large and small scissors, craft knife, pencil, ruler, and eraser.

Pencil lines, whether freehand or ruled, should be drawn on the right side of any paper or cardboard unless the project directions are otherwise. The lines are a guide for scissors or craft knife, and cutting from the right side prevents tearing that side of either paper or board.

Before cutting, straight lines are always measured with the ruler and *lightly* drawn with a pencil along the edge of the ruler.

Cutting Thin Papers

Use scissors to cut thin paper: drawing paper, typewriter paper, tissue, tracing, gift wrap, shelf paper, Con-Tact or other self-sticking papers. A craft knife will sometimes tear thin paper. With the scissors, follow pencil or felt-tipped pen lines very carefully, as the finished project depends on this first outline. If you have a small design with lots of ins and outs to cut, use small scissors. Large scissors are best for long straight lines or big shapes.

Cutting Art Boards or Cardboard

To begin with, put several thicknesses of newspaper under any paper board that is to be cut with a craft knife. This will keep the flat working surface from being cut.

Most boards made of paper are too heavy to be cut cleanly with scissors. These boards include cardboard (both plain and corrugated), illustration, poster, matting, and bristol. Bristol board is thin enough to be cut with large scissors *if* the design outline is curved, but sharp straight lines should be cut with a craft knife and ruler.

A craft knife, braced straight up against the ruler's edge, is the best cutting tool for all paper boards. For clean sharp edges, always cut on the right side of the board. If you cut from the back of the board, the front surface may tear a bit, spoiling a design.

When cutting through paper boards, draw the knife lightly alongside the edge of the ruler. Repeat the cut five or six times, adding a little more pressure each time until the board is cut through to the other side. If you try to cut through the thickness of the board in one try, you run the risk of slipping off the pencil line. The pressure will be too great on the knife point, making it hard to control.

If your design made of paper board needs a fold, the board is *scored* to make a sharp edge. Lay the ruler along the line on the side which will have the outward folded corner. Draw the craft knife lightly down the line, *once only*. Remove the ruler and gently ease both sides of the board away from the scored line until the correct angle is achieved.

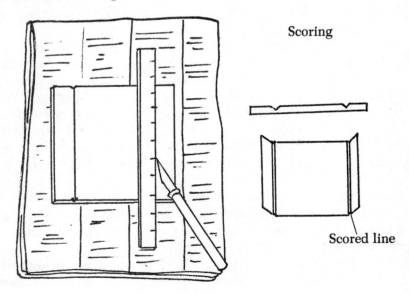

Scoring

Scored line

To cut a curved line with a craft knife requires patience and a steady hand. Carefully go over the line freehand many times as you slowly deepen the cut. It is better to make a few extra cuts than to have the knife slip and spoil the design.

Techniques of Gluing Paper and Board

Most of the projects in this book are held together with white household glue (such as Elmers). You will need: a small shallow plastic container to mix glue and water; a flat, ¾- to 1-inch wide watercolor brush; facial tissues; ruler; and lots of newspapers. Also have ready a small bowl of water in which to dip your fingers and brush as they get sticky, and plenty of paper towels for drying.

For most projects the glue is too thick to spread thinly and evenly over the paper or board. Squeeze glue into a small container and add a little water, drop by drop. Stir with the wooden end of the brush until it is the right thinness. Always use the flat soft brush to apply the glue to the paper.

When you are gluing a very thin piece of paper, like tissue paper, onto a heavier one, brush the glue on the heavier paper or board. If glue sinks in quickly, add a second coat; then lay the thinner piece of paper over the glue. Smooth from the center to the edges, patting lightly with a wad of facial tissues.

If the two papers are approximately the same weight, put glue on the back of the top sheet—or on both facing surfaces.

For a final smooth surface, "iron" the papers together. To do this, lay a sheet of typewriter paper over the newly glued papers. Draw the edge of a ruler firmly across the typewriter paper, from the center out to the edge. Be sure to brace the typewriter paper with your other hand at the opposite edge from the ruler's direction; this will keep the paper from slipping. Repeat the ironing motion toward the other three edges. Remove the typewriter paper and mop up any excess glue at the edges.

Ironing

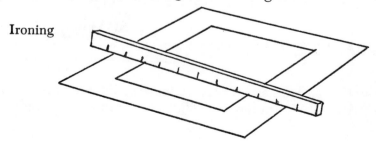

To keep glued papers from curling up while drying, put a heavy weight on top of the flat sheets; a phone book or several large books will do. Protect the surface with a clean sheet of paper. Leave the weight on until the glue is dry. This may take only a short time, or it can be a couple of hours or overnight; it all depends on how much glue was used and how dry or wet the weather is.

If you cannot use a weight on a glued section, such as the corner of a box, hold it in place with a large paper clip or a strip of masking tape.

Cardboard and heavier art boards will need glue applied to both facing surfaces and may need more than one coat, as the glue will sink in.

Wood glue should not be thinned out. Apply it to both facing surfaces of wood, or wood and paper, with a short narrow strip of cardboard. Put a weight on top until dry.

When applying Con-Tact paper or any other self-sticking paper, read the manufacturer's directions carefully. If you do get bubbles under the surface, the paper can be lifted and smoothed out. Apply the paper slowly, smoothing out as you go along, patting the surface with a wad of facial tissues. The main caution is not to stretch the paper. This can be prevented by removing the backing slowly as you work, rather than taking it off all at once.

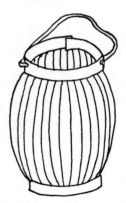

JAPANESE LANTERNS

Brightly-colored slashed paper lanterns hung around a room are easy decorations for a party. They are not made for candles, but their colors light up a room or a patio for a summer afternoon birthday party. Make them from construction paper in several sizes and colors. Tiny ones can be hung from a mobile form to sway in a breeze.

Materials and Tools
construction paper, any color
white household glue
thin string
pencil
ruler
scissors
craft knife
flat watercolor brush, 1 inch wide
small container for mixing glue

Directions
1. Measure and cut a strip of construction paper, 6 × 12 inches. On the right side of the paper, measure and lightly draw with pencil a ⅝-inch margin on each long edge. Starting at one short end, put a pencil dot every ½ inch on each margin line. Connect the dots on the two lines with light pencil lines drawn between them (see diagram).

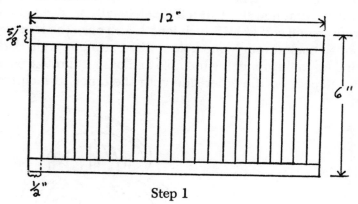

Step 1

2. Cut through the paper at each of these lines either with scissors or with a craft knife braced against a ruler. Do not cut through the margins.

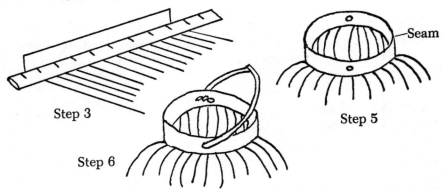

Step 3

Step 5

Step 6

3. Lay the ruler edge along one margin pencil line and bend the paper margin up so it is at a right angle. Repeat with the other margin.

4. Curve the lantern into a circle and glue the two short ends together, overlapping the last two ½-inch wide strips. Let dry.

5. With the seam on the right, punch two holes, opposite each other, in the top margin, using the point of the scissors.

6. Slip one end of an 18-inch length of string through one hole, from front to back, and tie the inside end in a knot. Repeat on the other side, pushing the other end of the string through the hole, front to back, and tying the end in a knot on the inside. Then hang up the lantern.

7. If you want a fat round lantern, also punch matching holes in the bottom margin. Cut a 30-inch length of string in half. Tie a knot in one end of a 15-inch length and poke the free end from front to back through one hole in the bottom margin. Bring the string up to the matching top hole and push it through to the outside. Repeat on the other side with the other 15-inch length of string.

Step 7

8. Place the palm of your hand on top of the lantern and press down lightly until the sides of the lantern bulge. When you are satisfied with the roundness of the lantern, tie a knot in each string on the outside of each upper hole. Tie the ends of the string together and hang up the lantern.

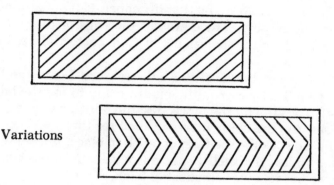

Variations

Variations: Instead of straight cuts, make slanting cuts, or V cuts, and then follow directions for making the lantern (see diagrams).

LABELS

This is a very easy project. Use small labels for your notebooks and bookcovers, a large size for a bookplate. Kitchen labels to identify jars of jam and jelly, spice jars, and storage containers for other foods make great gifts.

Materials and Tools
solid-color shelf paper or Con-Tact paper, ½ yard
stiff paper, 6 × 6 inches
white household glue
pencil
ruler
scissors
compass
felt-tipped black pen or black china marker pencil
flat watercolor brush, ¾ inch wide
small container for mixing glue

Directions

1. Labels can be any size you choose. Design your own or follow the measurements shown on the diagrams. You may want to make the labels all one shape, or make several of each shape. Use the compass for circles and half circles.

2. Make a pattern on the stiff paper. Cut out around the edges with the scissors. Trace around the edge of the pattern on the wrong side of the shelf paper or Con-Tact. Make as many labels as you need.

3. Cut out the labels with the scissors. Leave the backing on the Con-Tact paper until you are ready to use the labels.

4. To write on the labels, use the felt-tipped pen for the shelf paper; use the china marker pencil for the Con-Tact paper.

5. To stick the shelf paper labels in place, use white household glue, unless the shelf paper has a self-sticking back. Con-Tact paper has its own self-sticking back.

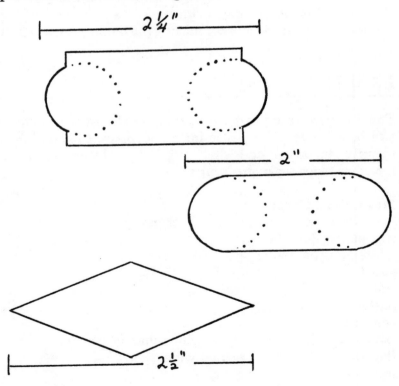

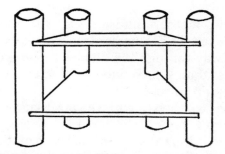

DESKTOP DISPLAY SHELVES

Make these quick shelves to show off a collection of small objects. Or turn the shelves into an open-air parking garage for small cars or a hangar for model airplanes. The cardboard tubes and the corrugated cardboard shelves can be left unfinished, or shellacked, or painted with acrylic polymer gloss medium. The shellacked base can be covered with enamel paint, and the gloss medium covered with acrylic paint. Con-Tact paper can also be used to cover tubes and shelves.

Materials and Tools
cardboard tubing: 4 pieces, 11 inches long and
   1½ inches in diameter (either mailing tubes
   or tubes from paper towels)
corrugated cardboard: 2 sheets, 10 × 12 inches,
   ⅛ inch thick
small can of shellac, and small can of
   enamel paint (optional);
   or acrylic polymer gloss medium, and
   tube of acrylic paint;
   or 1½ yards of Con-Tact paper
pencil
ruler
scissors
craft knife
flat watercolor brush, 1 inch wide
flat nylon brush, 1 inch wide
small container for mixing acrylic paint

Directions

1. With the craft knife, measure and cut two slits in each 11-inch long tube. Make each slit 2¾ inches from the end of the tube, cutting *almost* halfway through the diameter of the tube. Make these slits a little less than ⅛ inch wide, so that the shelves will be held in the slits by pressure.

2. Measure and cut the two shelves with the craft knife; each one is 10 × 12 inches.

3. If you are planning to finish the shelves and tubes with shellac, acrylic polymer gloss medium, enamel or acrylic paint, do this now, following directions in the section on painting (page 6).

4. If using Con-Tact, follow the manufacturer's directions for applying it to the tubes and shelves. Cut away the slit areas after the Con-Tact is in place on the tubes.

5. Slip the four points of the shelves into matching slits in the tubes, and the shelves are complete.

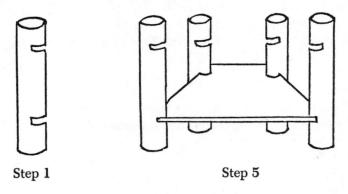

Step 1   Step 5

Variations: You may change the height measurement between the shelves to fit whatever objects you plan to display. Tubes can be longer; flat shelves can be larger.

CHRISTMAS TREE ORNAMENTS

Make your own Christmas tree ornaments: snowflakes, old-fashioned cornucopias, baskets, pleated fans, chains, a string of paper dolls. Use these, too, to decorate a wreath shape or to hang from mobiles. Cut the ornaments from foil wrapping paper in gold and silver, bright blue, green, or red. You can make decorations of one color, two colors, or all colors—it's your choice.

Materials and Tools
colored foil gift wrap paper, either rolls or folded sheets
typewriter paper
white glue
button thread, any color
pencil
ruler
scissors
craft knife
paper clips
flat watercolor brush, 1 inch wide
small container for mixing glue

Directions
Follow the measurements shown on the drawings, or enlarge any of the squared-off patterns by the grid method.

Snowflake: Cut out two squares of paper, 8½ × 8½ inches, or choose your own size. Glue the two wrong sides together with thinned-out white glue. Let dry.

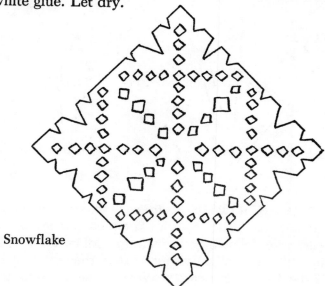

Snowflake

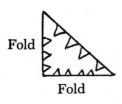

Fold

Fold

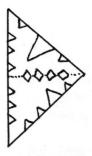

When the glued papers are dry, fold them in half, then in half again to form a square; then in half diagonally to form a triangle; and again in half to form a smaller triangle. With the scissors, cut out small triangles as shown on the diagram. Unfold the first triangle, and make two large triangle cuts as shown on the diagram. Unfold completely, and hang on the tree with thread attached to one of the points. Experiment with other folds and cuts.

Old-Fashioned Cornucopia: Cut one sheet of paper for each cornucopia, following the measurements given. Curve into a cone, and glue the edges together. Punch two holes in the back of the cornucopia at the top, and attach thread (see diagram). When filled with candies or nuts, tuck in the top triangle.

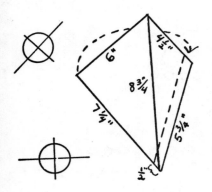

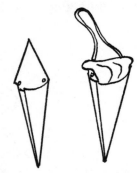

Old-Fashioned Cornucopia

Basket: Cut two shapes for each basket, following the measurements given. With the craft knife, cut slashes in each side of *one sheet only*, following the diagram. Cut twelve lengths of contrasting foil paper, slightly shorter than the length of each side, and ⅓ the depth of the slashes. Weave these strips through the slashes.

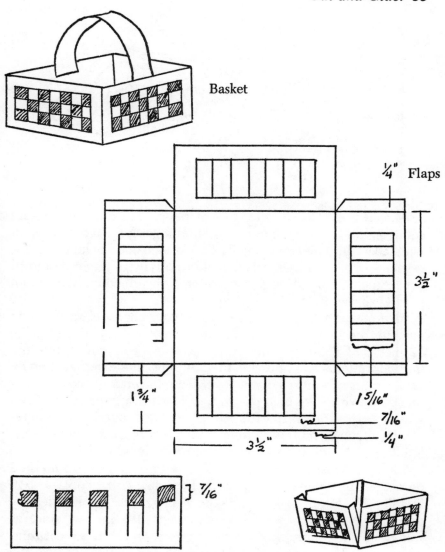

Basket

¼" Flaps

3½"

1¾"

1⁵⁄₁₆"

7⁄₁₆"

¼"

3½"

} 7⁄₁₆"

Hold the ends in place on the inside of the basket with white glue; let dry. Glue the two wrong sides of the basket shapes together. Let dry under a book. Fold the flaps in place, and glue down. Hold the glued flaps with paper clips until dry. Cut two handles and glue their wrong sides together. Attach to the basket with glue as shown in the diagram.

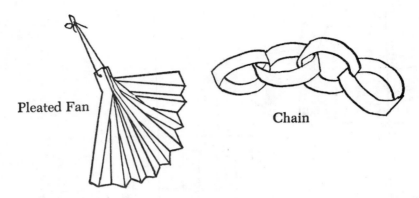

Pleated Fan

Chain

Pleated Fan: Cut two lengths of paper, same or contrasting color, 4 × 11 inches; glue wrong sides together. Fold in ½-inch wide accordian pleats. Bring ¾ inch of one end of the pleats together and glue to each other. Hold tightly with paper clip until dry. Punch a hole through the center of the glued end and run a loop of thread through the hole.

Chain: Cut as many narrow strips (your choice of size) as you need for the length of chain. Ten links ½ × 4½ inches will make 12 inches of chain. If you want both sides colored, double the number of foil strips and glue them wrong sides together, two by two. Colors can match or contrast. Glue the ends of the first ring together, with a ½ inch overlap; hold with a paper clip. Then loop a strip through the first ring; put ends together and glue. Continue until you have a long enough chain, or several chains, holding each link with a paper clip until the glue dries.

String of Paper Dolls: Enlarge the pattern by the grid method on a sheet of typewriter paper, and cut out. Cut two 21 × 5½ inch lengths of foil paper, and glue wrong sides together; let dry under heavy books. Fold into six pleats 3½ inches wide, as shown on the diagram. Place the pattern on the top pleat, and trace around the edges of the doll with the pencil. Be sure the outer edge of each hand is flush with the edges of the folded paper. Cut out around the outline, but *do not cut* the outer edge of each hand (the dolls are held together by the hands at each folded edge). Open up the string of six dolls; punch a hole in the heads of the two end dolls and the center one; slip a loop of thread through each hole.

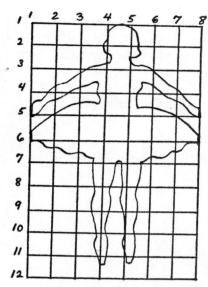

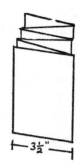

String of Paper Dolls

Enlarge to ½" squares

Variations: See Mobiles (page 8) for directions for making a wire form. Hang various ornaments on the form.

Bend a wire clothes hanger into a circle. Tie pine or spruce branches to the wire with thread or nylon wire. Add ornaments to the wreath with thread loops. Use the hanger hook to hang the wreath. Ornaments can also be added to a commercial wreath.

PICTURE PUZZLE

Picture puzzles are made from any picture in a magazine, a magazine cover, a colored print, or a family photograph, which is pasted on a sheet of illustration board or plain cardboard. The board is then cut into pieces—and you have a puzzle ready to put together. You can also make a frame to hold the puzzle in place.

Materials and Tools
colored magazine illustration, advertisement or cover;
   or art print;
   or family photograph
illustration board or plain cardboard, same size as picture
typewriter paper
white household glue
pencil
ruler
scissors
small container for mixing glue
flat watercolor brush, 1 inch wide
black felt-tipped pen with fine point
craft knife
facial tissues
newspapers

Directions
1. Trim the picture around all the edges so that no white paper shows. Measure and cut the illustration board or plain cardboard to the same size as the picture.
2. Mix white glue with a little water. With the brush, spread a thin coat of white glue over the surface of the illustration board or cardboard. Lay the back of the printed picture over the glue, and smooth it into place with a wad of tissues. Cover with a sheet or sheets of typewriter paper. Pull the edge of the ruler, held at a 45° angle, over the surface of the paper to smooth out any wrinkles. Hold the typewriter paper in place with the other hand. Use tissues to mop up any glue that was squeezed out. This is called "ironing." Let dry for several hours.
3. The next step is to cut the picture into pieces. With ruler and pencil, measure vertical and horizontal lines on the surface of the picture (see diagrams for suggested patterns). The size of the pieces depends on the size of the picture. Pieces should be a little larger or a little smaller than 1 inch on each side. For in-

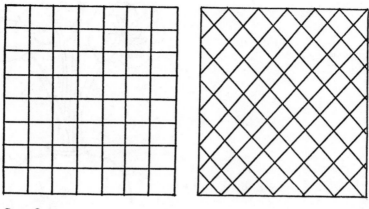

Step 3   Patterns

stance, if the picture is 8 × 10 inches, you will have even 1-inch squares; if 8½ × 10½ inches, the pieces will measure $1\frac{1}{16}$ × $1\frac{5}{16}$. (Pieces can also be different sizes.) Go over the lines with ruler and felt-tipped pen on the color side of the picture.

4. Cut out the pieces, placing the ruler on each line as a guide for the craft knife. (See directions for cutting cardboard, page 41.)

Warning: Put several thicknesses of newspaper under the illustration board or cardboard to protect the working surface from any cuts.

Variation: Cut the piece of illustration board 2 inches wider all around than the picture. After the picture is glued in place in the center of the board, cut it out along the edges, leaving a 2-inch wide frame all around. This will hold the puzzle in place as you put it together again.

SPLASHY PAPER FLOWERS

Make your own flowers at any time of the year. Fill a vase with tissue paper blooms of impossible sizes and wild colors: bright purple, vivid orange, magenta pink, emerald green, and madras stripes.

Materials and Tools
tissue paper, any colors
self-sticking tape, ¼ inch wide,
    medium or dark green
thin stiff wire
white household glue
pencil
ruler
scissors
wire cutter
round watercolor brush, #4
small container for mixing glue

Directions
1. In this project you'll make all the decisions: how large the flowers; how many shapes are used to form the flowers; how long

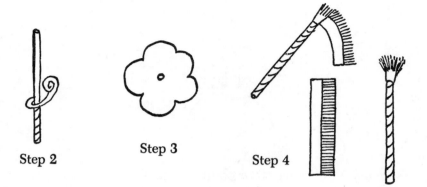

Step 2   Step 3   Step 4

the wire stems; and what colors or combination of colors. One suggestion is given here, and then you're on your own.

2. Cut off an 8-inch length of wire. If it seems too light, cut a second 8-inch length and twist the two wires together. Wrap the wire or wires with self-sticking tape in an overlapping, spiral pattern. Curl over ¼ inch of the top of the wrapped wire.

3. Cut five 3-inch wide rounded-petal flower shapes from orange tissue paper. Cut a strip of dark red tissue paper, 1 × 8 inches.

4. Make ¹⁄₁₆-inch wide cuts, ½ inch deep, on the 8-inch strip of red tissue paper. Lightly spread thinned-out glue on the uncut ½ inch. Put one end against the top ½ inch of the wire and roll it around and around until the whole length is wrapped around itself at the top of the wire (see diagram). Let dry.

5. Now push the five flower shapes up the length of the wire, one at a time. Try to alternate the petals of each shape (see diagram). Cup the five shapes around the center pompom and hold in place with the green tape.

6. Repeat with as many sizes and colors as you wish, until you have enough flowers for your vase.

Step 5

Variation

Variation: Put three or four pointed petal shapes on top of the five rounded petal shapes. Do not cup into an upright flower, but keep flower more open and flat. Or make the five petal shapes different sizes on one flower, smaller shapes on top of larger shapes.

LACE PAPER VALENTINES

Valentines are fun to make, especially when you can transform red construction paper and lace paper doilies into pretty cards for friends and relatives. Write your own message inside with a white pencil.

Materials and Tools
lace paper doilies, 12 inches in diameter
construction paper, red
typewriter paper
white pencil
white household glue
pencil
ruler
scissors
flat watercolor brush, 1 inch wide
small container for mixing glue

Directions

1. Fold the sheet of typewriter paper in half crosswise. Then measure and cut off 3 inches at the bottom of both halves. With the fold on the left, measure and draw a center line from top to bottom.

2. Draw a heart shape, using the center line as your guide. Let the curved line flatten for about 1¾ inches at the center of the fold. Cut out the heart, leaving the 1¾ inches on the fold uncut.

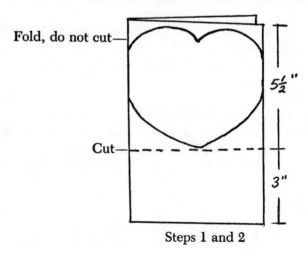

Steps 1 and 2

3. Trace around the edges of the heart on a matching folded sheet of red construction paper. Cut out with the scissors, again leaving the 1¾ inches on the fold uncut.

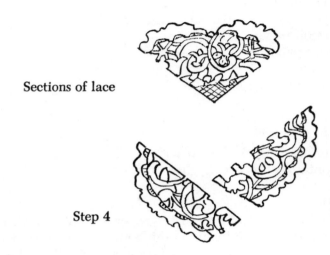

Sections of lace

Step 4

4. Decorate the front of the heart with sections of lace paper doilies, fitting sections together to cover the heart. Plan the sections so the ruffled edge of the doily becomes the edge of the heart. Glue the sections together, then glue the doily heart to the red paper one.

5. Cut out several small red hearts and paste them in the center area of the lace paper to hold the sections together.

6. With the white pencil, write your message on the inside of the card.

Variation: You can also make a large rectangular card. Fold a sheet of red construction paper in half, and trim it with lace paper. Cut paper in sections, gluing on several overlapping layers. The lace paper can also be pleated. Decorate the lace paper with several small red hearts.

CINDERELLA WALKING DOLL

Cinderella, running from the ball at midnight, lost one of her glass slippers. Push this walking doll across a table top, and you will see her run with one slippered foot and one stockinged foot.

Materials and Tools
bristol board, 9 × 9 inches, dull surface
typewriter paper
lead pencil transfer paper
acrylic or watercolor paints: white, red,
	yellow, and brown
colored crayon pencils (optional)
black felt-tipped waterproof pen
brass-colored paper fastener
pencil
ruler
scissors
thin nail
compass
flat nylon brush, ¾ inches wide
round nylon brushes, #3 and #5

Directions
   1. Enlarge the doll pattern and the leg circle by the grid method on the typewriter paper. Transfer doll and circle to the bristol board, using lead pencil transfer paper.
   2. With the felt-tipped pen, outline the figure and fill in the details of face, hair, and clothes. Outline *only* the legs and slipper on the circle. With the compass, go over the outside line of the circle so it is perfectly smooth and completely round.
   3. To color Cinderella's face, hair, hands, legs, and dress, follow Steps 5 to 8 for A Real Paper Doll (page 73).
   4. When all the paint is dry, cut around the outlines of the doll and circle with the scissors. Be sure there are no flat sections along the edge of the circle.
   5. Make a hole in the dress with the point of the scissors, the compass, or a thin nail (see diagram marked A). Make another hole in the center of the circle (see diagram marked B). Holes should be made from front to back so no rough edges show on the painted surface. Enlarge each hole by twisting the paper fastener around, so the circle will move freely; trim edges of paper.
   6. Slip the pointed end of the paper fastener through the hole in the dress, from front to back. Then slip the points through the center hole in the circle, from front to back. Put the doll, face

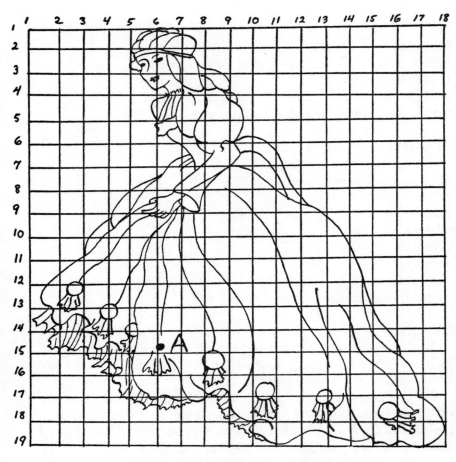

Enlarge to ¼ " or ½ " squares

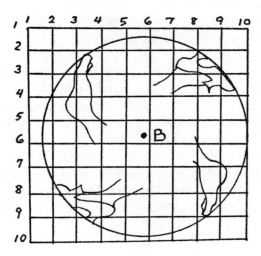

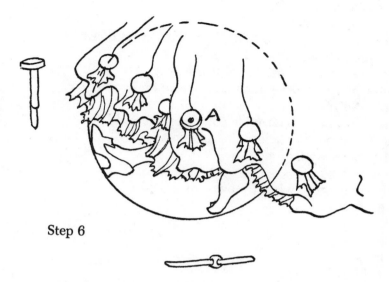

Step 6

down, on a flat surface; pull the ends of the fastener apart and spread the metal strips flat against the circle. Test to make sure the circle will move freely.

7. Hold the doll upright so the bottom edge of the circle touches a table top. Push Cinderella over the flat surface and you will see her running legs as she dashes for her coach.

Variation: You can also make a ragged dress to go over the ball gown by following directions for A Real Paper Doll (page 72).

COLORFUL PICTURE FRAMING MATS

Paper mats to separate a picture from its frame are easy to make, and they give a professional look to framed pictures. Mats may be made from white or colored matting board, poster board, or illustration board. There are many ways to decorate the surface of the mat, and some of these are described in the steps of this project; you will invent many more ways. Always plan your mat to complement the picture, not to overwhelm it.

Materials and Tools
picture and frame
matting board, poster board, or illustration board,
    white or colored
gift wrap paper, colored or silver or gold
poster paint: two 1-ounce jars, white and color
    of your choice
masking tape, 1 inch wide, black or colored
labeling tape, ¼ inch wide, any color
white household glue
brown paper
picture hanging wire, up-eyes, and hooks
small brads
pencil
ruler
scissors
craft knife
wide-toothed comb
flat watercolor brush, 1 inch wide
small containers for glue and paint

Directions
  1. Choose a picture and frame. The frame should be large
enough to allow for a mat between the picture's edge and the inner
edge of the frame.
  2. Turn the frame over to the back. Around the edge of the
opening is a small shelf on which the outer edges of the mat will
rest. Measure from one outside edge of the shelf to the other, top
to bottom and side to side, for the overall size of the mat (see
diagram).

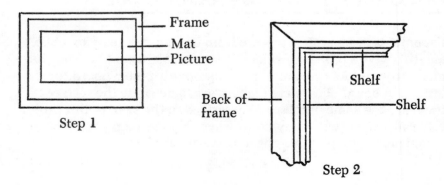

Frame
Mat
Picture
Step 1

Shelf
Back of
frame
Shelf
Step 2

3. Mat proportions may vary from picture to picture and frame to frame. Here is a good general rule: the bottom is the widest; the top is narrower than the bottom but wider than the sides; the two sides are the narrowest. Another method is to make all four sides the same width. This style is often used if the frame is very narrow and the picture very small, but you want an important-looking framed picture.

4. Sometimes the mat becomes both frame and mat. Back up the mat with a same-size, solid piece of the same type of board, sandwiching the picture between backing and mat. Hold the picture in place with a drop of glue at each corner. Attach the mat to the backing with masking tape folded over the edge—half in front, half in back. This will take the place of a frame. You can also add a sheet of glass or clear plastic cut to the same size as the mat; hold glass, mat, and backing all together with the tape.

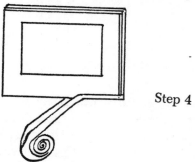

Step 4

5. If you want to design special mats, here are some suggestions.
   a. Brush poster paint thinly over white illustration board.
   b. Put on light-colored poster paint very thickly; then, before it dries, comb it in a wavy pattern with a wide-toothed comb. This can be done over a darker, contrasting color of board.
   c. Make two mats, one larger than the other, in contrasting posterboard colors. One or both of these mats can also be covered with fabric, such as thin silk or velveteen.
   d. Glue gold or silver gift wrapping paper to white illustration board. Add one or two lines of ⅛-inch wide tape in a contrasting color around the inside edge of the mat.
   e. Trim a plain colored mat with decoupage cutouts or narrow tape.

f. Make marbled paper—see Printed Papers (page 36) for directions.

g. Cover the inside edge of a plain mat with gold or silver paint.

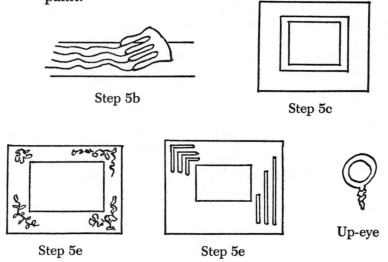

Step 5b

Step 5c

Step 5e

Step 5e

Up-eye

6. To finish framing the picture, attach the picture to the mat with masking tape. Cover the back with a sheet of plain cardboard or the matting material, the same size as the mat. Hold in place in the frame with small brads or the clips that are attached to some frames. Glue a sheet of brown paper over the back, brushing the glue onto the back of the frame. This will protect the picture and mat from dust. Put an up-eye screw on each side of the frame, ¼ of the way from the top, and attach the wire. Hang the picture on a wall hook.

EVERLASTING WALL CALENDAR

Make a wall calendar that never goes out of date from four heavy paper egg cartons, plus a sheet of illustration board. The cartons can be painted with acrylic or poster paint or left unpainted. The months and days are on separate tags that can be moved around.

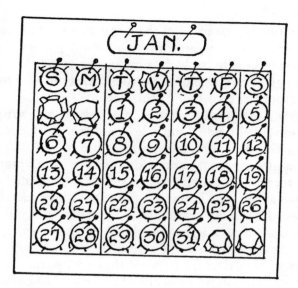

Materials and Tools

4 egg cartons

illustration board, 16¼ × 16½ inches (see Step 3)

white bristol board or colored poster board,
    11 × 13 inches

white household glue

tube of acrylic paint or jar of poster paint (optional),
    any color

acrylic polymer gloss medium (optional)

40 ball-headed pins with colored tops, 1½ inches long

stick-on picture hanging rings (optional)

felt-tipped pen, any color

cord for hanging calendar

pencil

ruler

scissors

craft knife

compass

flat watercolor brush, ¾ inch wide

flat nylon brush, 1 inch wide

small plastic containers for glue and paint

paper punch

Directions

1. Cut off the covers from the egg cartons, using the ruler as a straight edge for the craft knife. Cut away part of the long flap on the opposite side, so as to remove the two "closing" bumps. Cut one egg carton in half lengthwise. Cut out two separate egg holders from the flap half of this carton.

2. On a flat working surface, place the three cartons and the half carton side by side, long sides touching. Each cut side should overlap a flap side (see diagram).

3. Measure the length and width of the carton square. To these measurements add 1 inch on each side, 1 inch at the bottom, and 3½ inches at the top. This is the size of the illustration board base.

4. Measure the illustration board and cut with the craft knife. Measure and draw a light pencil line on the board as a guide in placing the cartons for final gluing.

5. If you have decided to paint the cartons, now is the time to do it. Paint the bottom projections and their background, *except*

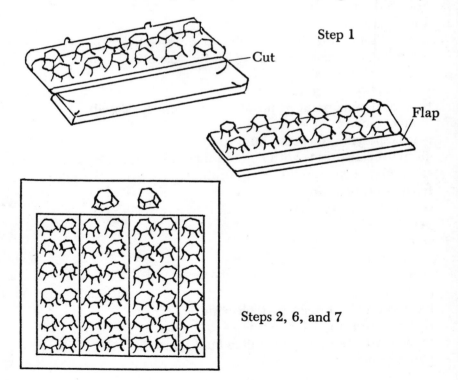

Step 1

Cut

Flap

Steps 2, 6, and 7

the side flaps. Let them dry. You can add a coat of acrylic polymer gloss medium on top of the paint for a high gloss. Use the nylon brush for both.

6. Glue the cartons to the background board. The first carton is placed at the left, the flap to the right. The straight edge of the next carton covers the flap; its flap is also to the right. Add the third carton, then the half (unflapped) carton in the same way.

7. Center and glue the two separate egg holders ½ inch above the top edge of the cartons and with ½ inch space between them.

8. Lay heavy books or telephone books over the top of the egg cartons until the glue is dry.

9. With the compass draw 38 circles, 1½ inches in diameter, on the bristol board; allow ⅛ inch between circles. Cut out with the scissors. On seven of the circles put the initials of the days of the week—S, M, T, W, T, F, S—using the felt-tipped pen. Number the remaining circles from 1 to 31.

Steps 9 and 10

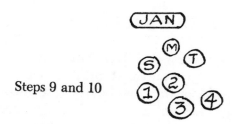

10. Measure and cut twelve oblong tags, 1½ × 3 inches, from the bristol board. Print the abbreviated names of the months on the tags with the felt-tipped pen.

11. Punch a hole in the top of each round and oblong tag.

12. When the glue is dry, punch a hole in each top corner of the illustration board, or add stick-on picture hanging rings to the inside top corners of the board. Tie the hanging cord to the holes or rings.

13. Stick a ball-headed pin through the top front edge of each projection. (You can buy these pins in small boxes at the dime store.) On the top row, hang the days of the week circles on the pins. Then, starting with the correct day of the week, add the date numbered tags. On the double top projection hang the name

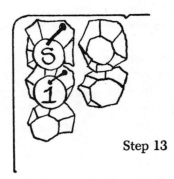

Step 13

of the month. Each month, change the name and the position of the numbers.

Variation: You can use colored poster board instead of bristol board for the round and oblong tags.

A REAL PAPER DOLL

Make your own paper doll from stiff bristol board, with clothes made from drawing paper or printed paper. Her clothes can match your own, or they can be drawn from your imagination. Look in magazines and store catalogs for ideas for your doll's everyday and party clothes—plus a Halloween costume or ballet dress.

Materials and Tools
bristol board, 9 × 9 inches, dull surface
drawing paper, 8 × 15 inches for four outfits
4 sheets of typewriter paper
1 sheet of lead pencil transfer paper
tubes of acrylic or watercolor paint: white, black,
    brown, red, yellow, and blue (other colors optional)
white household glue (optional)
colored crayon pencils
pencil
ruler
scissors

waterproof felt-tipped pen, thin point
small plastic containers or paint mixing tray
round nylon brushes, #3 and #5

Directions

1. Enlarge the doll pattern by the grid method on a sheet of typewriter paper. Transfer it to the bristol board, using lead pencil transfer paper.

2. Repeat with the clothes, enlarging them on separate sheets of typewriter paper. Transfer to the drawing paper with lead pencil transfer paper.

3. With the waterproof felt-tipped pen, follow the outline of the doll and fill in the face, hair, underwear, and shoes.

4. With the waterproof felt-tipped pen, outline the clothes and fill in their details.

5. Color the doll with acrylic or watercolor paint.

   a. Paint the face, arms, and legs flesh color. Squeeze about ½ inch of white paint into the mixing dish or tray, adding enough water to make a thin mixture. Add the tiniest bit of red paint on the tip of the #5 brush and mix well. Then add the same amount of yellow. Add a little brown if you want a darker tone. Try the color on a scrap of bristol board and let dry. If it is the right color, paint face, arms, and legs. Let dry. (If the color is not right, adjust with white, brown, red, or yellow.) Add color to the eyes and lips, as well as the hair.

   b. Underwear can be left white or you can color it.

   c. Paint shoes either black or brown.

6. Paint the clothes any color you want, always thinning out the paint with water so the color flows on evenly. The more water, the lighter the color. For very pale colors, add some white paint. Always let paint dry before adding another color on top of the first coat or beside it.

7. The doll and clothes can also be colored with colored crayon pencils.

8. When the doll and clothes are dry, cut them out along the outlines with the scissors.

9. Fold over the tabs and try on all the clothes.

10. You can use these patterns as the base for other clothes; or

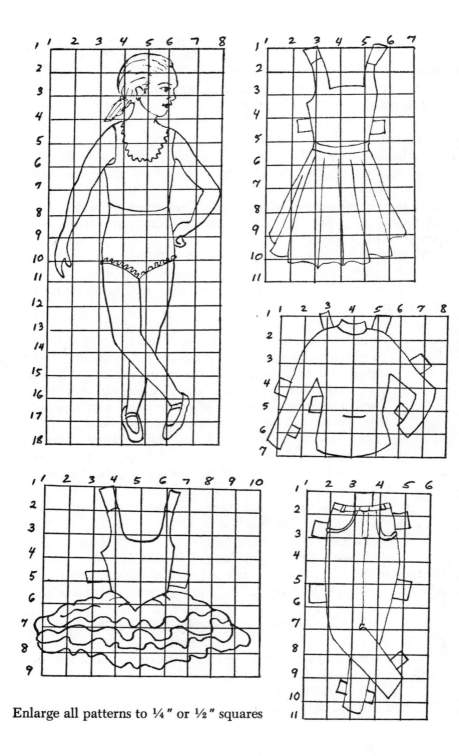

Enlarge all patterns to ¼" or ½" squares

make your own patterns by tracing around the edges of the doll.

Warning: Always paint clothes before cutting them out; then the paper will not curl up because of the wet paint.

Variations: You can make party dresses from tissue paper. Finely pleat a skirt and glue it to a basic drawing paper pattern which is plain or colored. Cut out the top of dress from tissue paper. If this is a costume, you can add gold sprinkles or sequins held in place with drops of glue. You can also make dresses from tiny-patterned or plain printed papers; trim them with narrow bands of colored tape.

Make a whole family of dolls, or a group of friends. You can also trace a figure in a catalog or magazine and enlarge it by the grid method onto bristol board.

Collage and Decoupage

Techniques of Working With Collage and Decoupage

Collage and decoupage are standard craft words, as no single word in English describes either of these two processes. There is a slight difference in the meaning of these two French words, even though both refer to the cutting and gluing of printed designs (or sometimes shapes of colored paper) to a sheet of paper or a solid object.

Collage means "pasting or gluing paper." As a craft term it refers to a collection of cut-out pictures which, when put together, form a new design. For instance, you might combine a picture of a tropical beach, an out-of-proportion shell drawing overlapping one edge and several fish and/or tropical flowers trailing off on the other side. This collection forms a new picture that shows the many parts of a tropical world.

Decoupage means the "art of cutting out." It refers to a single cut-out picture which is applied to an object as a decoration. This printed picture can be a squared-off scene, a cut-out flower or fruit design, or any other single picture. For instance, a recipe

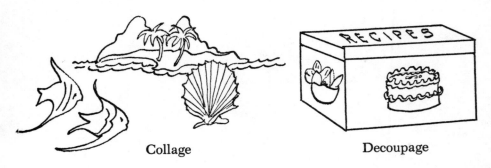

Collage   Decoupage

box might be decorated with a picture of a cake on the front, a salad on one side, a roast on the other side, and a steaming plate of spaghetti on the back.

Both of these techniques became very popular in France in the eighteenth century when court ladies decorated furniture and small objects in imitation of the popular hand-painted Italian furniture. And this craft is still popular all over the world.

Look in magazines for useful illustrations or advertisements; seed catalogs have colored pictures of flowers and vegetables; gift wrap paper and wallpaper both have interesting designs which can be cut out; and then there are family and friends' photographs which can be used.

For cutting and gluing directions, read the section on techniques of cutting and gluing paper (pages 41–44). The only difference is that glue is applied to the cut-out paper design, which is then pressed against the heavier object and "ironed" into place.

DECOUPAGE SERVING TRAY

Make one-of-a-kind trays from plain ones of plastic, metal, wood, or fine straw by adding your own decoupage designs. Cut out appropriate printed designs; create a wood-grained effect; or make a cut-out design from plain colored tissue paper.

Materials and Tools
tray: metal, plastic, wood, or fine straw,
    your choice of size and color
wallpaper, print, magazine illustration, wood-grained
    or plain Con-Tact, or tissue paper
white glue
acrylic paint (optional)
acrylic polymer gloss medium
paste wax (optional)
pencil
ruler
scissors
flat watercolor brush, 1 inch wide
flat nylon brush, ¾ inch wide
facial tissues

Directions for Printed Picture Tray

1. Wash and dry the tray to remove any dirt or grease.

2. Cut out around the edges of a wallpaper design, illustration, or print. Place the design on the surface of the tray, and use a pencil to lightly mark on the tray the top, bottom, and sides of the design shape.

Cut-out design

3. Lightly cover the back of the paper design with thinned-out white glue, using the watercolor brush.

4. Turn the design over and place it within the pencil marks on the tray. Smooth with a wad of crumpled face tissues. Iron with the edge of the ruler. Wipe off any glue which oozes out along the edges. Let dry for several hours. Wash out the brush.

5. When it is dry, cover the printed material with a thin coat of acrylic polymer gloss medium, using the ¾-inch nylon brush. Let it dry, then add a second coat if needed.

Directions for Wood-grained Tray Design

1. Measure the tray bottom; divide the length and width into equal 1-inch, 1¼-inch, or 1½-inch square measurements. The size of the squares depends on the size of the tray. If the tray measurement is an uneven size, plan to add a border all around of the same material or contrasting color (see diagram).

2. Turn wood-grained Con-Tact over to the paper-backing side. Measure and draw the size of the tray bottom. Then measure and rule the separate squares. Next, measure and rule the border if needed, either from the wood-grained Con-Tact or a leftover solid color Con-Tact paper. You can also paint a border with acrylic paints.

3. Cut out the square pieces, laying them temporarily in place on the tray as you cut them. As you put down each piece, change

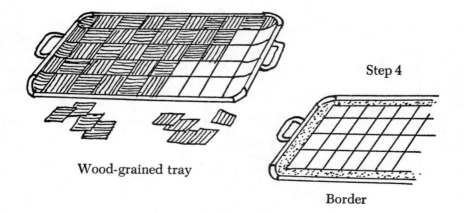

Step 4

Wood-grained tray

Border

the direction of the wood grain, alternating the direction on each row. This will give the effect of a parquet wood floor or a woven surface (see diagram).

4. Put the border in place if needed. Peel off the backing and press into place.

5. Now, starting at one corner, carefully peel off the paper backing of the first square. Press into place. Continue until all the squares are in place.

6. The Con-Tact surface can be left as is, or covered with acrylic polymer gloss medium or with paste wax rubbed on gently.

Directions for Watermelon Tray

1. From red, white, and green tissue paper, cut out a quarter watermelon shape. Glue it carefully to a white metal or plastic tray (see gluing directions, page 43).

2. When it is dry, cover with acrylic polymer gloss medium. You can also cut out other fruit and vegetable shapes as tray decorations.

Watermelon tray

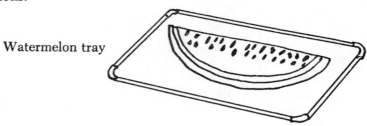

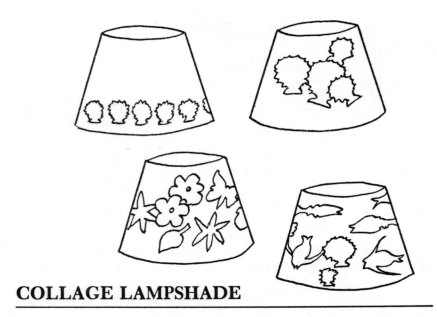

COLLAGE LAMPSHADE

Make a plain white lampshade more interesting with a collage decoration; either decorate one already in the house (ask permission first) or buy a new one. Cut shapes in several sizes from colored tissue paper or painted rice paper: long triangles, fish, scallop shells, flower and leaf shapes, butterflies, starfish, seaweed. These can be glued around the edge of a shade, in an all-over pattern, or in groups. The fish or scallops can be connected with seaweed shapes, and the flowers with real strands of dried grass.

Materials and Tools
lampshade, white or a very light color
colored tissue or rice paper
typewriter paper
white household glue
pencil
ruler
scissors
flat watercolor brush, 1 inch wide
small container for mixing glue
facial tissues

Directions

1. Make a freehand enlargement of the shape or shapes of your choice on the typewriter paper. Cut out the pattern with the scissors. Trace around the edges on the tissue or rice paper, making as many copies as you need. You can make several sizes, or make the shapes in different colors. You can also draw your own shapes.

Step 1

2. Arrange the shapes in a design that you like: overlapping each other; scattered singly or in clusters around the shade; in one big design on one side; in a border around the bottom edge; or in combinations of two shapes, such as fish and shells or flowers and butterflies.

3. Make light pencil dots on the shade as a guide to the final placement of the shapes.

4. Mix glue with a little water. With the watercolor brush, add glue to the shade between the pencil marks. Press the paper designs in place with a wad of facial tissues.

5. When it is dry, place the lampshade over a light bulb.

Variation: You can use this same design to decorate a window shade (see Picture Window Shades, page 82) or a wastepaper basket (see Gifts With Decoupage Decorations, page 85).

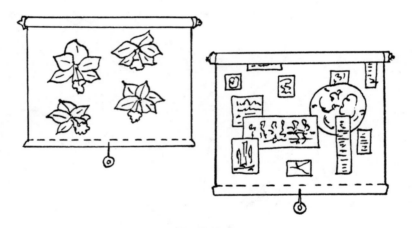

PICTURE WINDOW SHADES

A plain white window shade can be made into a pretty decoration by gluing cut-out designs to the room-side surface. Match the wallpaper or add contrasting designs for a plain-walled room. You can use the shade as a "memory gallery," adding photographs, prints, or clippings from magazines or newspapers that have a special meaning for you.

Materials and Tools
white or pale colored window shade
wallpaper, colored paper, prints, photographs, etc.
white household glue
pencil
ruler
scissors
flat watercolor brush, 1 inch wide
small container for mixing glue
facial tissues
newspapers

Directions
   1. Cover a floor area with newspapers. Stretch the window
shade flat on the floor, room side facing up. Hold in place with
books along the edges.
   2. Cut out designs and place them in position, marking along
the outside edges with light pencil dots. Remove designs; brush
thinned-out glue over their backs and press them into position on
the shade (see gluing, page 43). Let dry before putting shade into
position on the window frame.

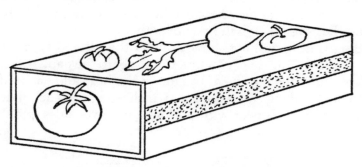

LARGE KITCHEN MATCHBOX

Cover a large box of kitchen safety matches as a gift for someone
who has a gas stove, a fireplace, or an outdoor barbecue. Use solid
color Con-Tact or construction paper, and decorate with cut-outs
of fruits or vegetables: for the barbecue, a steak or frankfurters;
for the fireplace, something that goes with the living room style.

Materials and Tools
large box of kitchen safety matches,
    approximately 4¾ × 2⅝ × 1½ inches
white Con-Tact paper, ½ yard, and
    solid color Con-Tact paper, ½ yard;
    or construction paper, 8½ × 11 inches
small designs cut from wallpaper, magazines,
    or other printed papers
white household glue
pencil
ruler
scissors
flat watercolor brush, 1 inch wide
small container for mixing glue
facial tissues
newspapers

Directions
   1. Since ½ yard is the smallest amount of Con-Tact paper you can buy, look through this book for other uses of Con-Tact, and buy a color that can be used in other projects.
   Most boxes of matches have bright advertising material printed on the cover. You will first cover the box with white Con-Tact so the printing will not show through the colored Con-Tact.
   2. Turn the sheet of white Con-Tact to the paper side. Measure and draw the outline of the top of the box; add each side, down to the "striking" area. Add a ½-inch margin at each short end for a turn-over. Repeat with bottom and lower sides (see diagram).

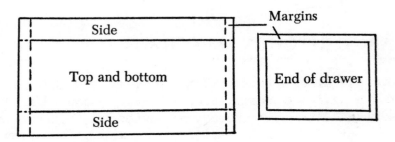

Step 2

3. Cut out the two rectangles.

4. Center the top half of the white Con-Tact on the box so the two "striking" areas are not covered. Crease along the two top edges. Starting at one long end, peel off the backing paper according to manufacturer's directions. Smooth Con-Tact into place.

5. Repeat on the bottom of the box.

6. Repeat Steps 2, 3, 4, and 5 with the solid colored Con-Tact. Or just leave the box covered with the white Con-Tact, depending on your design.

7. Cover the ends of the drawer, first with white, then with the colored Con-Tact (see diagram). Fold a ½-inch margin of paper over the sides, trimming the corners to make a neat finish.

8. If you are using construction paper instead of Con-Tact, follow directions in Steps 2, 3, and 7 for covering the box and drawer ends. You do not need the white Con-Tact; construction paper is heavy enough to cover the printing on the box. Use thinned-out white glue to hold the paper in place.

9. Add cut-out decoupage decorations to the top of the box and the ends of the drawer. Use white glue, applied with the flat brush.

Variation: You can use shiny gift wrap paper or shelf paper in place of construction paper.

GIFTS WITH DECOUPAGE DECORATIONS

For parents or other relatives, or for friends, decorate gifts with decoupage designs: a tissue box, a wastepaper basket, a clothes hamper, kitchen canisters, a metal cookie box. Use leftover wallpaper if the room the gift will be in is papered. If the walls are plain, pick a design that goes with the room color or that reflects a hobby or special interest.

Materials and Tools
tissue box, metal wastepaper basket, hamper,
    metal canisters, or metal cookie box
wallpaper, colored or black-and-white prints,
    or magazine cut-outs

Con-Tact paper, amount and color to fit
   your project (optional)
white household glue
acrylic polymer gloss medium
pencil
ruler
scissors
flat watercolor brush, 1 inch wide
flat nylon brush, ¾ inch wide
facial tissues

Directions

   1. If you cannot find a tissue box, wastepaper basket, or canisters of the right background color, cover them with Con-Tact paper. Follow the manufacturer's directions for measuring, cutting, and applying the paper to your project.

   2. Cut out the design and decide just where it should be placed, and mark the area with pencil dots at the top, side, and bottom edges of the picture.

   3. With the watercolor brush, lightly cover the back of the cut-out paper design with thinned-out white glue. Apply the design to the object, keeping it within the pencil dots. Smooth into place with a wad of face tissues, mopping up any extra glue around the edges.

4. Let stand until glue is well dried (several hours or overnight).

5. With the nylon brush, cover the decoration with one or two coats of acrylic polymer gloss medium, letting dry between coats.

MEMO PAD AND ADDRESS BOOK

As gifts to yourself or a friend, glue plain or printed paper to the stiff covers of memo pads or address books; decorate them with cut-out designs or labels. Personal telephone books or notebooks can be covered in the same way. Their "spines" are covered with wide, solid-color tape, and the corners can also be covered with tape.

Materials and Tools
memo pads, address books, telephone number books,
    notebooks (solid back or spiral binding)
plain or printed shelf paper, gift wrap, Con-Tact,
    or tissue paper
wallpaper, prints, or magazine advertisements
self-sticking tape, any width and color
white household glue
pencil
ruler
scissors
flat watercolor brush, 1 inch wide
container for mixing glue
facial tissues

Directions
1. On both sides of the stiff covers of a memo pad, glue decorative or plain paper, or make your own printed paper. On the outside, allow a ½-inch turnover on three sides. On the inside of the cover, glue a sheet of paper the same size as the stiff cover. Repeat on the back cover.

2. The folded edge of the pad, called the "spine," is covered with tape; the tape reaches over to the front and back covers. Do not cover a spiral-bound spine (see diagram).

3. You can add a label in the center of the front cover (see

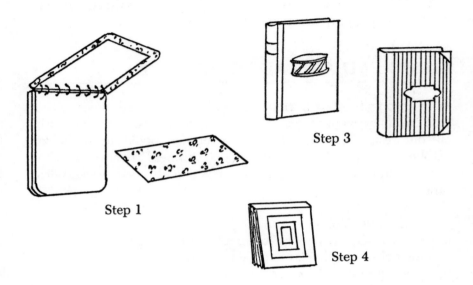

Step 1

Step 3

Step 4

Labels, page 47). If the background is plain paper, add a cut-out decoupage decoration.

4. The same covering method is used for an address book, personal telephone book, or a school notebook. On these larger, stiffer covers, try a decoration of tissue paper over a plain color covering. Add several layers of different colors, slightly overlapping each other, to form a framing mat, with a small picture in the center (see drawing).

5. The corners of the books can be covered with the same tape you used on the spine.

SMALL TABLE SCREEN

The Chinese and Japanese have always made small folded table screens in a plain color or decorated with a scene. These are used to set off a pretty bowl, a flower arrangement, a plant, or a small carved figure or animal. They are easy to make from illustration board or cardboard, covered with solid-color gift wrap paper and decorated with decoupage cut-outs.

Materials and Tools
illustration board or cardboard, 8 × 12 inches
gift wrap paper: gold, silver, black, or color
oriental designs from wallpaper, catalogs, gift cards,
    or advertisements
self-sticking tape, ⅝ inch wide, black or color
white household glue
pencil
ruler
scissors
craft knife
flat watercolor brush, 1 inch wide
small container for mixing glue
facial tissues

Directions
    1. Divide the sheet of illustration board or cardboard into three pieces, each one 4 inches wide and 8 inches deep. Draw pencil lines, and cut with the craft knife, using the ruler as a straight-edge guide for the knife.
    2. Measure and cut out six pieces of the colored paper, 4 × 8 inches.
    3. With the flat brush, spread a thin coat of thinned-out glue on one side of a section of illustration board or cardboard. Cover with one of the pieces of paper. Smooth with a wad of facial tissues, then iron with the edge of the ruler (see gluing, page 43). Repeat until one side of each of the three sections is covered.

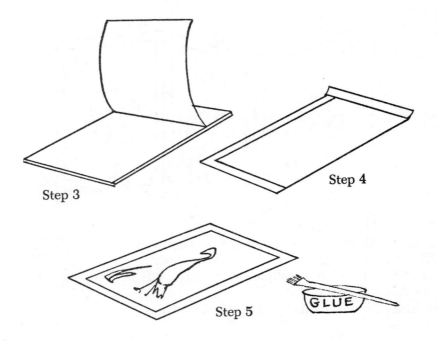

Step 3

Step 4

Step 5

GLUE

Then turn the sections over and repeat the gluing process with the other three sheets of paper. Let all three sections dry with books on top of them. Wash out the brush and container.

4. When dry, cover all edges with the self-sticking tape. Fold tape in half over the edges, cutting the corners at an angle.

5. Cut out the decoupage designs and glue them to the panels. Let dry, weighed down with a heavy book.

6. To join the three pieces together, put them side-by-side with ⅛ inch of space between the long sides. Cut four strips of tape, 8 inches long. Very carefully, join the first and second panel with one strip of tape, being sure that the even line at the bottom is not disturbed, nor the space between the two pieces. You might try lining up the bottoms of the two panels along the edge of the ruler. Repeat, joining the third panel to the second one with a piece of tape. Turn over the three joined pieces and repeat the joining of the first and second, and the second and third panels.

7. Stand the screen on a flat surface, and bend the joined panels into a shallow zig-zag so the screen will stand alone.

Step 6

Variation: You can make a screen with four, five, or six folds instead of this three-fold.

ORIENTAL PENCIL HOLDER

This holder is six-sided, a design shape popular in China and Japan. It is like a six-sided screen brought together at the ends, with a piece to close off the bottom. Cover it in shiny paper in black, gold or silver, or a color, and trim with oriental-style decoupage cut-outs.

Materials and Tools
illustration board, 6 × 15 inches and 6 × 6 inches
shiny gift wrap paper: gold, silver, black, or a color
wallpaper or other printed designs
self-sticking tape, ½ inch wide, color or black
white household glue
pencil
ruler
scissors
craft knife
flat watercolor brush, 1 inch wide
small container for mixing glue
facial tissues

Directions
1. On the right side of the illustration board, measure six sections, each one 2½ × 6 inches. Draw light pencil lines, then score along these lines with the craft knife, using the ruler as a straight edge.

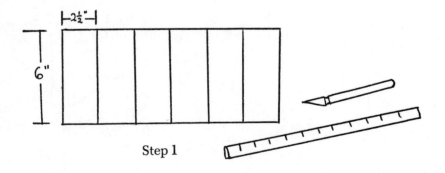

Step 1

2. Measure and cut twelve pieces of shiny paper with the scissors, each one 2½ × 6 inches.
3. Glue six pieces to the right side of the illustration board, and the other six pieces to the wrong side, using thinned-out

white glue (see gluing, page 43). Let dry under a heavy book.

4. Glue a small design on the right side of each panel. Or, if you have a long narrow design, cut it into six pieces, and glue separate pieces on each section. Let dry.

5. Fold the illustration board along the five scored lines. Hold the two ends together with a 6-inch length of colored tape centered over the seam. Then cut five more 6-inch lengths of tape. Center each piece of tape over the outside of a scored fold. You will now have a six-sided tube.

6. Place the tube upright on the 6 × 6-inch piece of illustration board. With a pencil, draw around the outside edge. Cut along the pencil lines with the craft knife, using the ruler as a cutting edge. Cover both sides of this six-sided piece of board with the shiny paper, gluing it in place with the thinned-out white glue. Let dry under a heavy book.

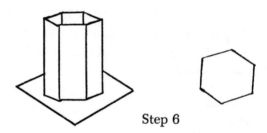

Step 6

7. Cut six lengths of tape, each one 2½ inches long. Lay the six-sided piece flat on the working surface. Attach ¼ inch of the width of each length of tape to the outside *bottom* of the six-sided piece. Place the tube upright over the flat piece, and turn the tape up around the sides of the tube.

8. Cover the top edge of the tube with tape, centering the tape along the edge. Cut either six pieces, 2½ inches long, or one long piece around the edge.

9. Fill the holder with pencils or pens and put it on your desk.

Variation: Make a six-sided tube large enough to slip over a round waste-paper basket, then add the bottom. Or use heavier card-

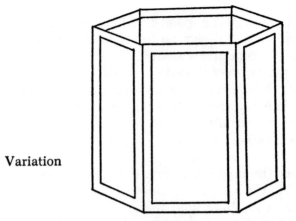

Variation

board to make a free-standing wastepaper basket in this same design.

SUMMER FAN

This is a simple project to make a hot summer day comfortable. Let yourself go with bright colors and decorations in either decoupage or collage designs.

Materials and Tools
typewriter paper
bristol board, 8 × 15 inches
bright color tissue paper, solid color Con-Tact,
    or construction paper, 8 × 15 inches
self-sticking tape, ¾ inch wide,
    black or color
wooden dowel, ½ × ¼ × 16 inches,
    or half circle ½ × 16 inches
magazine advertisement, seed catalog picture,
    print, postcard, photographs
small bottle of hobby enamel, black
    or color to match tape
white household glue
wood glue
pencil

ruler
scissors
craft saw
small container for mixing white glue
flat watercolor brush, 1 inch wide
facial tissues

Directions

1. Cut the dowel so you have two pieces, each 8 inches long. Paint one broad side of each dowel with the black or colored enamel. Also paint the two narrow sides with enamel; or the curved side of the half-circle dowel. You will have to add a second coat after the first one has dried. Leave one flat side on each dowel unpainted. The unpainted sides will be glued together to form the complete handle.

2. Enlarge the fan pattern by the grid method on the typewriter paper. Cut out the enlarged pattern with scissors and place on a sheet of bristol board. Trace around the edges with a pencil; then trace a second shape on the bristol board. Cut out both shapes with the scissors. (Keep the pattern—see Step 10.)

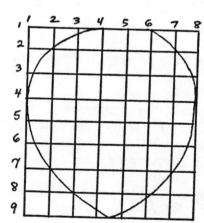

Enlarge to 1″ squares

3. Spread thinned-out white glue with the 1-inch brush on one side of each bristol board shape. Put the glued sides together. Place a heavy book on top until the glue is dry; this takes at least two or three hours. Wash out the container and brush.

4. If you are using tissue paper to cover the surface of the fan, cut out two shapes the same size as the fan by tracing around the edges of the bristol board shape.

5. Spread a *thin* coat of thinned-out white glue on one side of the bristol board. Carefully lay one piece of tissue paper over the glue. Gently pat it into place with a wad of facial tissues, using an up-and-down movement. When the glue is dry, turn the fan over, and repeat with the other piece of tissue paper. Let dry. If you want a deeper color, repeat the process with a second layer of paper over the first piece of paper.

6. If you are using Con-Tact, cut out two pieces, the same size and shape as the fan. Follow the manufacturer's directions for applying the paper to the fan shape.

7. If you are using construction paper, follow the directions in Steps 4 and 5.

8. Cover the edges of the fan with self-sticking tape, so one-half of the width of the tape is on each side of the edge.

9. Now you are ready to decorate the center of the fan with either a decoupage or collage design, on one side or both sides. Here are several suggestions; the final choice depends on what cut-out materials are available. Remember that the handle will cover an area 3 inches long and ½ inch wide at the bottom of the fan.

> *a.* A series of fan shapes in different colors of tissue or construction paper, overlapping each other and getting smaller and smaller by 1 inch.
>
> *b.* A small print in the center of the fan.
>
> *c.* Several pictures cut from magazines that suggest summer fun, a day at the beach, or a trip to the mountains. Put them together, overlapping the edges to form a summertime collage picture.
>
> *d.* Family photographs or photographs of friends, cut out and formed into a collage picture—perhaps a great picnic, or a day at camp, or a block party.
>
> *e.* Small drawings or prints of flowers cut out from wallpaper or a seed catalog. Scatter them over the surface of the fan.

10. The last step is adding the already enameled handle. First, fold the paper pattern in half from bottom to top. Lay this over

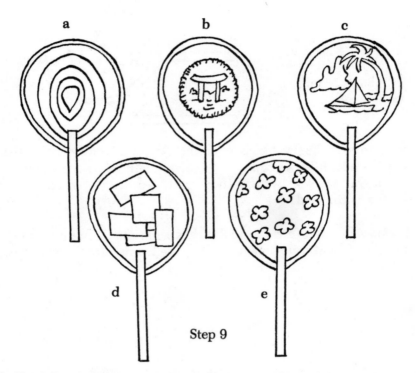

Step 9

half of the fan. Starting at the bottom, draw a very light line along the fold, 3 inches long. Do this on both sides of the fan. Remove the pattern. Then measure and draw two parallel lines, ¼ inch on each side of the center line and 3 inches long. Repeat on the other side of the fan. This is the guide for gluing on the handle.

11. Turn one dowel over to the unpainted side. Measure 3 inches from one end and draw a pencil line. Cover this 3-inch area with wood glue, using a strip of bristol board ½ inch wide and 2 inches long as a spreader. Turn the dowel over and carefully place it on the fan between the parallel pencil marks. Place a heavy book on top until the glue is dry.

12. When the glue is dry, turn the fan over to the other side. Spread wood glue over the unpainted surface of the glued-on dowel. Then spread glue over the whole unpainted surface of the other dowel. Place this one over the fan and dowel already in

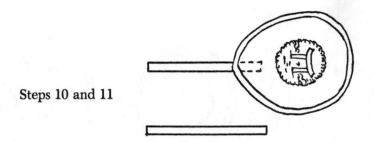

Steps 10 and 11

position. Put heavy books over the dowels, being careful that they do not shift position. Wipe off any glue that oozes out between the dowels. Let dry thoroughly—overnight is best. Now the fan is finished.

Variation: Small fans 1½ to 2 inches wide can be hung on a wire mobile. (See Mobiles, page 8, for wire frame directions.)

Papier-Mâché

Techniques of Working With Papier-Mâché

Because small boxes and bowls and other objects made from papier-mâché were popular in France in the eighteenth century, this inexpensive molding method still carries its French name. The name translates into minced or mashed paper. The insides of old boxes were often unfinished, so that one can still read the news of the period from the newspaper strips.

Today there are two craft methods of making papier-mâché objects. One is the classic method, using strips of newspaper dipped into flour and water paste. The other uses a dry paper-pulp mixture to which water is added until the material can be smoothed on, like clay, to the mold form.

Newspaper Strips

Cut or tear ½- to 1-inch wide strips of newspaper, the full length of a newspaper page. Cut some of the strips in half crosswise. Set aside.

Next make a flour and water paste in a small bowl, using ½ cup of flour and ¼ cup of water. Slowly stir the water into the flour, smoothing out any lumps. Add 1 tablespoon of white glue, and mix well. Slowly add more water, if needed, to make a thin paste.

Spoon some of the paste into a wide, shallow bowl or dish. Pass strips of newspaper through the paste one at a time, and transfer to the mold. Press each one smoothly around the mold surface. Build up the papier-mâché to a thickness of ⅛ to ¼ inch as you criss-cross the paste-soaked strips of paper over the mold. Keep a

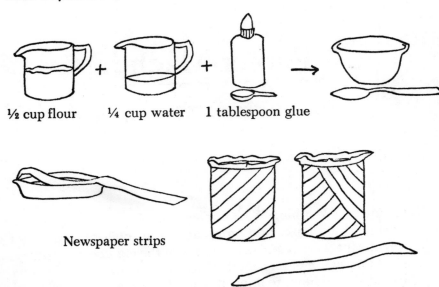

½ cup flour   ¼ cup water   1 tablespoon glue

Newspaper strips

bowl of water handy, plus paper towels, so that as you work you can wash the paste off your hands and dry them. When finished, set the object aside until almost dry, then remove it from the mold.

Instant Papier-Mâché

A papier-mâché pulp mixture is sold in 1-pound packages in craft or art stores. The very fine gray powder is mixed with water, following the manufacturer's directions. The current products do not contain asbestos. You may be able to make several projects from one package.

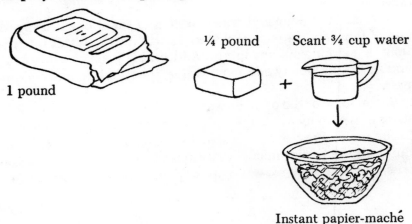

1 pound   ¼ pound   Scant ¾ cup water

Instant papier-mâché

Applying instant papier-mâché

The papier-mâché paste is spread over a plastic-wrap-covered mold with your fingers, a flat metal spatula, a table knife, or a flat wooden stick. Allow papier-mâché to almost dry before removing it from the mold. Once dry, it is treated just like the newspaper strip papier-mâché.

Types of Molds

You will find many objects around the house to use as molds: a straight-sided glass, a small flower pot, a saucer, a smooth-sided bowl, a balloon, a bottle, butternut squash or other squash shapes, or hard-skinned fruits. Look around and you'll find many more objects you can use as molds for papier-mâché projects.

Removing a Papier-Mâché Form From a Mold

The simplest molds from which to remove papier-mâché forms are a straight-sided glass, a saucer, a small flower pot, a smooth-sided bowl, and a balloon. The first four should be covered with plastic wrap before applying papier-mâché. The papier-mâché form, partially dried, can just be slipped off. A balloon can be left inside the papier-mâché object, or pricked with a pin and then pulled out through a small opening. Let papier-mâché dry thoroughly, sometimes up to one or two days.

If you completely cover a mold that is thicker or larger in some areas, then the papier-mâché form cannot be pulled off at all. A bottle and a butternut squash are two examples. There are two ways to remove this kind of form from a mold.

One way is to cut down each side and around the bottom, using a craft knife. Then carefully remove each side from the mold (see diagram, steps 1–3).

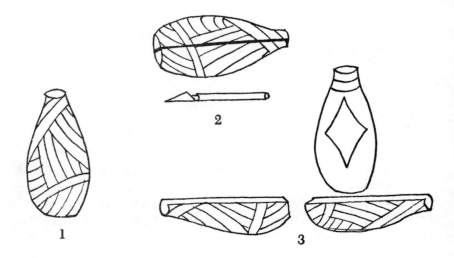

The other way is to apply a thin line of rubber cement down each side of the mold and across the bottom before you begin. Press a length of cord into the rubber cement, and let dry. Then bring the papier-mâché strips or pulp mixture up to each side of the cord, but not across it. When the covering is almost dry, pull the cord off the mold, and the two papier-mâché halves can be removed easily (see diagram, steps 4–6).

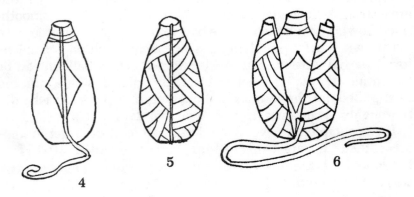

To put the object together again, add a line of unthinned white glue along the edges of the papier-mâché halves. Press

7   8

them together and hold in place with rubber bands until dry. Then criss-cross two more layers of newspaper strips or pulp over the whole form, covering the seam and blending out onto the rest of the object (see diagram, steps 7–8). Let dry.

Finishing a Papier-Mâché Form

When the papier-mâche form is dry, lightly sandpaper the surface, smoothing the edges of the paper strips or the rough surface of the pulp. Dust off with a soft brush. Cover the surface with shellac or acrylic polymer gloss medium. Let dry. You may need two coats. Paint with enamel or acrylic paints (see Painting, page 6, for complete directions).

BOTTLE SHAPES

Use a glass or plastic bottle as a mold for a papier-mâché bottle which can be painted in a bright color. Add your own label, a cut-out picture, or a painted design. Use the bottle to hold dried grasses or seed pods; or line up several shapes on a shelf as decorations. You can also cover straight-sided jars or drinking glasses with papier-mâché. When you remove the glass, paint the outside and inside of the container with acrylic paint and fill it with pencils, pens, or brushes.

Materials and Tools
glass or plastic bottle, or straight-sided
   drinking glass, any size or shape
newspapers

flour and water paste
white household glue
rubber bands
sandpaper
acrylic polymer gloss medium
tube of acrylic paint, any color
label or printed design (optional)
pencil
ruler
scissors
craft knife
flat nylon brush, ¾ inch wide
round nylon brush, #4
small container for mixing paint

Directions

1. First, read the section at the beginning of this chapter on preparing and applying papier-mâché.

2. Apply the paste-moistened newspaper strips to the outside of the bottle. Build up the paper to a ¼-inch thickness. Let dry.

3. At this point you can either leave the bottle inside the papier-mâché covering, or you can cut a lengthwise line down each side of the bottle and then across the center of the bottom. Remove the bottle. Cover the cut surfaces with unthinned white glue, and press the two halves together. Hold with rubber bands until the glue dries. Add two or three layers of newspaper strips to the seam and across the surface of the papier-maché bottle. Let dry.

4. Sandpaper the surface so it is smooth, then dust off with a brush.

5. Cover with acrylic polymer gloss medium, then with acrylic paint. Use the ¾-inch brush for covering large areas, the #4 brush for any details. (See directions for mixing and applying paints at the beginning of the book.)

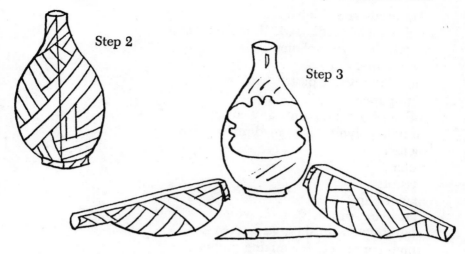

Step 2

Step 3

6. When paint is dry, put dry grasses or stems with seed pods into the top opening of the bottle as a final decorative touch.

Variations: A final coat of acrylic polymer gloss medium will give the bottle a high shine.

Make a large label for the bottle or cut out a printed picture as a decoration.

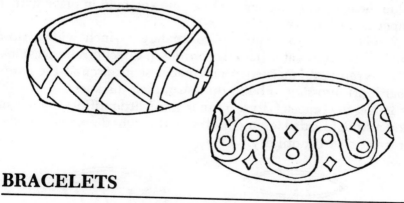

BRACELETS

For generations, papier-mâché jewelry has been made and worn in India and the Far East. Bracelets are easy to make and can be painted in bright designs. They can be made in any width from ¼-inch bangles to broad 3-inch cuff bracelets.

Materials and Tools
lightweight cardboard, 10 inches long,
    width of your choice
newspaper
flour and water paste
sandpaper
tubes of acrylic paint, any colors
acrylic polymer gloss medium
pencil
ruler
scissors
paper clip
flat nylon brush, ¾ inch wide
round nylon brushes, #2 and #4
small containers for mixing paints

Directions
   1. Curve the strip of lightweight cardboard into a circle. The circle should be large enough to slip easily over your hand when the fingers are held close together. Then open the circle just a bit more to allow for the thickness of the papier-mâché covering. Trim off extra cardboard at each end, leaving a ½-inch overlap. Glue the ends together with white glue and hold in place with a paper clip until dry.
   2. Cut newspaper into approximately ½-inch wide strips. Make flour and water paste according to directions on page 99.
   3. Wrap paste-moistened newspaper strips around the cardboard, crisscrossing to build up to a ⅛-inch thickness.
   4. Let the bracelet dry a bit so it gets a little stiffer. If you can find a straight-sided jar or glass that is the right diameter, slip the bracelet over it until dry.

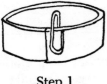

Step 1

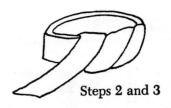

Steps 2 and 3

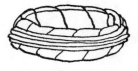

Step 5

5. Now cut narrower strips of newspaper, the width of the bracelet. Pull them through the paste and wrap them around the bracelet, building up the outside. Then add several rows of even narrower strips, until you are down to strips ⅛-inch wide. This will give your bracelet a slightly rounded top. Let it dry, on one edge if you do not have a jar or glass to hold it. Reform the circle if it is out of shape.

6. When it is thoroughly dry, sandpaper the surface to smooth it.

7. Add a coat of acrylic polymer gloss medium to both the outside and inside of the bracelet. Let dry. Add a second coat if needed. Use the ¾-inch flat brush.

8. Mix acrylic paint for your base color. Put on the base coat with the round #4 brush; let dry; add a second coat; let dry. You may want to wear this as a solid color bracelet, or you can add a design in one or more colors. See drawings for suggested designs. When paint is well dried, add a final coat of acrylic polymer gloss medium for a high shine. Let dry before wearing.

Variation: If you have some instant papier-mâché pulp, you can use it to add a high dome on the bracelet base. Leave it smooth, or cut a design into the pulp while it is damp, or add a raised design.

COLOR NECKLACE

Large lightweight beads are easily formed from instant papier-mâché. Make these in round, oval, or rectangular shapes, and paint them in bright colors

Materials and Tools
instant papier-mâché, 16-ounce package
plastic bag
tubes of acrylic paint: turquoise blue,
    purple, black, and white
acrylic polymer gloss medium
button thread or bead-stringing thread
sandpaper
pencil
ruler
scissors
tools for mixing instant papier-mâché
    (see manufacturer's directions)
round toothpicks
large-eye needle
round nylon brush, #4
small containers for mixing paint
8 small jam jars

Directions
1. Mix instant papier-mâché pulp with water, according to the manufacturer's directions.
2. With your hands, form ten rectangular beads, ¾ inch long and ⅜ inch wide, with slightly rounded edges at each end. Make nine round beads, ¾ inch in diameter, slightly flattened at each end. Make 20 round beads, a little larger than ¼ inch in diameter. Make 40 small round beads about half the size of the ¼-inch beads. With a round toothpick, make a hole through the center of each bead; the holes are lengthwise on the rectangular beads. Let the beads dry.

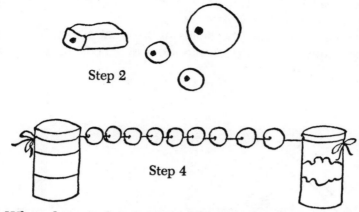

Step 2

Step 4

3. When dry, sandpaper all the beads to smooth the surface.

4. The next step is to paint the beads. First, string a length of button thread between two jars, tying it to the first jar. Add the ten rectangular beads to the thread, well separated. Tie the other end of the thread to the second jar. Move the jars apart to tighten the thread, and the beads will stay separated. Repeat with the other jars, thread, and beads, each one holding a separate shape.

5. Cover all the beads with the acrylic polymer gloss medium, using the nylon brush. Let dry. Add a second coat if needed.

6. Paint the rectangular beads with white acrylic; the large round beads with turquoise blue mixed with white; the smaller round beads a pale lavender (purple mixed with white); the smallest round beads with black. Let dry. Add a second coat if needed. Let dry. Add small and large splotches of full color turquoise blue to the rectangular beads. Let dry.

7. Cover the rectangular beads, the round lavender beads, and the small round black beads with acrylic polymer gloss medium. Do not cover the large turquoise blue beads. Let dry.

8. When dry, string beads on white button thread or bead-stringing thread. Start with one black bead; then one lavender bead; one black; one rectangle; one black; one lavender; one black; one large turquoise blue; then repeat, starting with the small black bead. When all the beads have been strung, tie the thread into a knot and cut off the ends; the necklace will be long enough to go over your head. Or you can add a metal clasp at the ends.

Variations: You can substitute small black plastic or glass beads for the tiny papier-mâché ones.

You can also paint the beads in different colors. Try making other shapes and other combinations of shapes, or all one shape for a necklace.

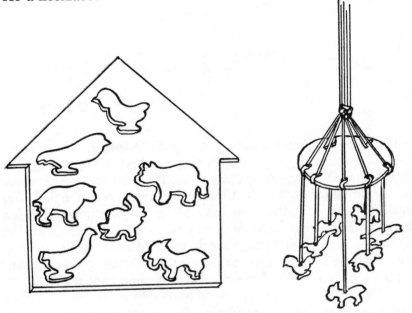

ANIMAL COOKIE MOBILE OR POSTER

Small animal-shaped cookie cutters are filled with instant papier-mâché pulp. When dry, the shapes are painted and hung from a mobile form made from wire coat hangers or a cardboard circle. Any shape cookie cutter can be used instead of animal shapes; round shapes can be painted with faces, suns, or flower designs. A barn-shaped poster covered with cookie shapes can be hung on the wall.

Materials and Tools
instant papier-mâché, 16-ounce package
wax paper
cookie cutters, animal or other shapes
acrylic polymer gloss medium

thin cardboard
tubes of acrylic paints, your choice of colors
2 wire coat hangers,
 or cardboard circle, 4 or 5 inches in diameter
self-sticking tape, ½ inch wide, black
black button thread or thin white string
pencil
ruler
scissors
thin nail
large needle
tools for mixing instant papier-mâché
 (see manufacturer's directions)
wire clippers
flat nylon brush, ¾ inch wide
round nylon brush, #2
small containers for mixing paint
poster board, your choice of size and color (for poster)
white household glue (for poster)

Directions

1. To mix the instant papier-mâché pulp, read the manufacturer's directions on the package and follow them very carefully. Collect all the tools needed before you begin the project.

2. Put a piece of wax paper on your working surface. From the thin cardboard, cut pieces to fit the cookie cutters and place them inside the cutters. Place the cookie cutters on the wax paper, then fill them to a ¼-inch depth with the papier-mâché mixture. Smooth the top so it is level. With the nail, make a hole right through the cookie on a "center" line ¼ inch in from the top edge.

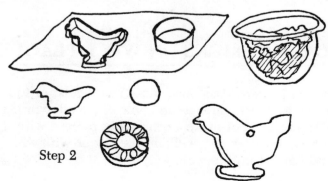

Step 2

3. When dry, remove cookies from the cutters. Cover top surfaces and sides with acrylic polymer gloss medium, using the ¾-inch nylon brush. Let dry, then turn the cookies over, and cover the cardboard side. Let dry.

4. Paint the cookies with acrylic paints and the ¾-inch nylon brush. First paint one flat surface and sides. Let dry. Turn over and paint the other side. Let dry. If the cookies need a second coat of paint, repeat the process. Add any extra decorations with contrasting colors, using the #2 nylon brush. For a very high gloss, you can finish with a covering coat of acrylic polymer gloss medium.

5. While the paint is drying, make either the metal clothes hanger or cardboard circle mobile form (see directions, page 8).

6. Push one end of the button thread or thin string through the hole in one of the cookies; tie it at the top of the cookie, then cut off a length of the thread or string. Repeat with all the cookies. The threads should be different lengths. Tie the other ends of the threads to the metal clothes hanger mobile, holding them in place with pieces of tape wrapped around both wire and threads. Or attach the cookies to the cardboard circle mobile with thread or string.

7. Hang the mobile from a center light fixture, in an open doorway, or over your desk.

Variation: The farm poster is made of red poster board cut in the shape of a barn. Enlarge the drawing by the grid method, or draw a barn shape freehand. Cookie animals can be painted white, or their natural colors (underside left unpainted); then they are glued to the board. When glue is dry, hang the poster on the wall.

CONCAVE DESIGNS ON WALL PLAQUES

Using instant papier-mâché mix, make rectangular or square wall plaques. Press objects, such as an apple or a scallop or clam shell into the top surface; or make a continuous pattern with the head of a meat tenderizer or grater. Paint the plaque with white acrylic paint and hang it on the wall.

Materials and Tools

instant papier-mâché, 16-ounce package
lightweight cardboard box, ¾ inch deep,
　　approximately 7 × 7 or 8½ × 5 inches
wax paper
apple, sea shell, meat tenderizer, or
　　other mold-making objects (see Step 4)
tube of acrylic paint, white
acrylic polymer gloss medium
sandpaper
white household glue
illustration board or cardboard,
　　same size as cardboard box
typewriter paper
self-sticking tape or masking tape,
　　white, 1 inch wide
2 stick-on picture-hanging hooks
picture wire
pencil
ruler
scissors
craft knife
materials and tools for mixing instant papier-mâché
　　(see manufacturer's directions)
flat nylon brush, 1 inch wide
small container for mixing paint

Directions

1. To mix the instant papier-mâché, read the manufacturer's directions on the package and follow them exactly.

2. If you cannot find a ¾-inch deep box, then cut down the sides of a deeper one. The cover of a box is often the right depth. Line the box neatly with wax paper.

3. Fill the box with papier-mâché pulp. Smooth the top even with the top edge of the box by drawing the ruler edge over it.

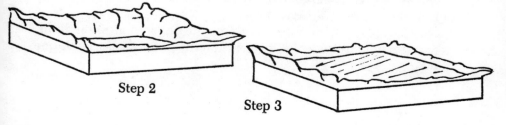

Step 2

Step 3

4. Press the object to be molded into the center of the plaque. For an apple, roll it a bit from side to side. You may have to scoop out a bit of the pulp before pressing the apple into the center of the plaque. With the point of the scissors, scoop out a stem shape at the top of the apple design. You also can use a large seashell, such as a scallop or a clam, pressed firmly into the center, or a row of smaller shells across the middle of the plaque. Or press an unshelled walnut into the pulp, forming a line of half walnuts. A knife, fork, or spoon can also serve as mold-makers, alone or together. If you use a meat-tenderizer, make an all-over pattern, matching the points as you repeat the pattern; or leave the center plain; or draw a ruled line between each impression. Look around the house or kitchen for other molding materials.

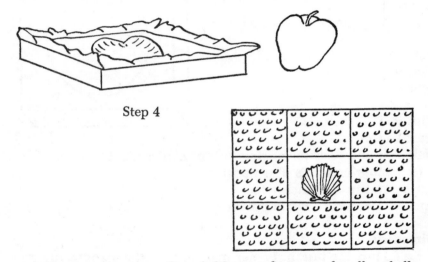

Step 4

Step 4, Meat tenderizer and scallop shell

5. Let the papier-mâché dry a bit; then carefully remove the plaque from the box by lifting up the sides of the wax paper. Place the plaque, decorated side up, on a metal cake rack. Let dry thoroughly.

6. When dry, sandpaper all surfaces to remove any rough spots, and dust with a soft brush.

7. Cover the top and sides with acrylic polymer gloss medium, using the nylon brush. Let dry. When dry, turn over the plaque and paint the lower surface; let dry. You may have to add a second coat; if so, repeat the process.

8. Next, cover the top and sides with white acrylic paint, using the nylon brush. Let dry, then turn plaque over and paint the other side. Let dry before adding a second coat of white acrylic. (See page 6 for complete directions for Steps 7 and 8.)

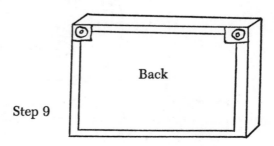

Step 9

Back

9. With the craft knife, cut a piece of illustration board or cardboard the exact size of the plaque. Spread thinned-out white glue over both the back of the illustration board or cardboard and the back of the plaque. Place the two glued surfaces together; lay a clean sheet of paper over the top of the plaque; put a heavy book on top of the paper until the glue dries.

10. Cover the sides of the plaque with the white self-sticking tape or masking tape, turning the extra ¼ inch over onto the board backing.

11. Press stick-on loops to the two top corners of the backing. Run picture wire through the loops; twist each end to fasten; hang the plaque on a wall hook.

Variations: The plaque can be painted any solid color, or the designs can be painted in a second color. Also, you can first cover the papier-mâché with shellac, then use enamel or flat paint.

ORIENTAL HOLLOW GOURD

A classic oriental pottery shape is a hollow gourd similar to a butternut squash. Part of one side is cut away in a circle or oval shape, and a small scene is placed inside. Make the same design in papier-

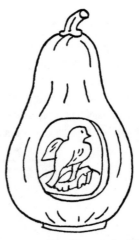

mâché, using a squash as the basic mold. On a shelf inside, put small china figures, tiny dried flowers, or a special keepsake.

Materials and Tools
butternut squash, 8 to 10 inches tall
newspapers
flour and water paste
typewriter paper
lightweight cardboard, approximately 6 × 6 inches
rubber bands
white household glue
masking tape, 1 inch wide
sandpaper
acrylic polymer gloss medium
tubes of acrylic paint: white, yellow, orange,
    brown, and blue
small decorations or figures
pencil
ruler
scissors
craft knife
flat nylon brush, 1 inch wide
small containers for mixing glue and paint

Directions
1. Read the directions in the beginning of the chapter for mixing flour and water paste and applying paste-soaked strips of

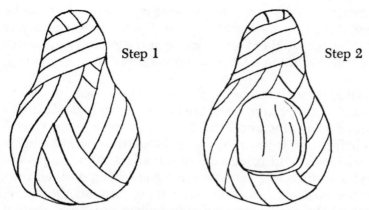

Step 1   Step 2

newspaper to the butternut squash. Build up the papier-mâché covering to a thickness of ¼ inch and let dry.

2. Cut away an oval opening on one side of the lower half of the papier-mâché squash. Size depends on the size of the squash. The drawing shows the approximate shape and proportions in relation to a squash. Draw the shape with a pencil on the papier-mâché; then cut it out with the craft knife. This opening will become the front of the papier-mâché squash shape.

3. Cut the papier-mâché covering of the squash in half lengthwise along two sides and across the bottom, using the craft knife. Remove the two sides from the squash mold. Cover the long cut edges with white glue and press them together. Put rubber bands around the top and bottom area to hold the halves together until dry.

Step 3

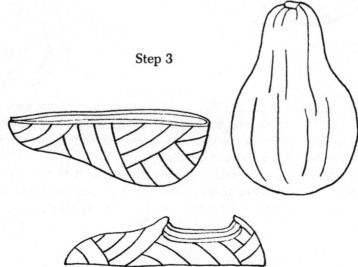

4. When glue is dry, add two or three layers of papier-mâché strips to seal the side and bottom seams. Spread them out across the squash surface so there is no seam mark. Also add extra strips to the bottom to flatten it. Add a short, curved stem at the top. Let dry.

5. To fit a flat shelf inside the papier-mâché squash just below the opening, cut a pattern from the typewriter paper. This will take a bit of measuring and fitting; you may have to cut several patterns before one is just right. Lay the pattern over the lightweight cardboard and trace around the edges with the pencil. Then add a ½-inch edging. Cut along the edging outline; then cut into the edging at ¼-inch intervals all around the circle, right back to the shelf pattern line (see diagram). Fold the cut edge upward, and brush the outside of the ¼-inch edging with white glue. Place shelf inside the papier-mâché squash, ¼ inch below the bottom of the opening. Press the cut pieces of the edging against the inside of the squash form. Tape in place if necessary. Let dry.

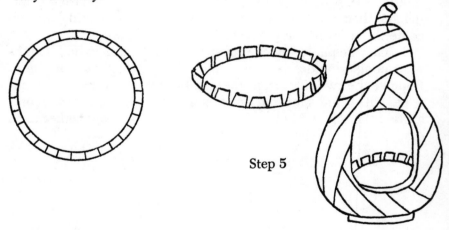

Step 5

6. When the glue is dry, add three or more layers of papier-mâché strips to the top of the shelf. Bring the ends of the strips up the inside wall to cover the cut edges of the shelf, and to smooth out the joining area. Let dry.

7. Smooth inside and outside surfaces with the sandpaper.

8. Cover surfaces inside and out with acrylic polymer gloss medium. Let dry. Add a second coat if necessary.

9. Mix orange paint with a little yellow and brown and cover the outside of the papier-mâché gourd. Let dry, then add a second coat of paint if needed. Let dry. Paint the stem light green: white with blue and yellow mixed into it.

10. Mix white with the yellow paint, and just a little of the orange color. Paint the inside of the gourd and the shelf surface. Let dry, then add a second coat. Let dry.

11. Put your treasured small objects on the shelf inside the gourd and display it proudly on a table.

PICTURE EGG

Hard egg-shaped shells of crystallized sugar trimmed with hard, white icing were originally made in Germany at Eastertime. Inside was a small scene, lighted from a small opening above and viewed through a hole at the narrow end of the egg.

In this project, the picture egg is made from papier-mâché, formed over a balloon; the mountain scene is made from molded and painted papier-mâché.

Materials and Tools
balloon, 4 inches long (before blowing)
newspaper
flour and water paste
white household glue

strip of thin cardboard, 1 inch wide
   (see Step 8 for length)
sandpaper
rubber cement
heavy cord, approximately 18 inches long
   (see Step 2 for length)
acrylic polymer gloss medium
tubes of acrylic paint: white, yellow, red, and blue
pencil
ruler
scissors
black felt-tipped marking pen
flat nylon brush, 1 inch wide
round nylon brushes, #2 and #4
small containers for mixing paint

Directions

1. Blow up the balloon until it is 8 inches long. Tie a piece of string around the neck. Use jars to brace the balloon with its neck up, then fill the neck with white glue. Let dry for several hours. This will hold the air in the balloon while you are working with the papier-mâché.

Step 1

2. Apply a ¼-inch strip of rubber cement around the balloon to divide it in half horizontally. Press the heavy cord into the glue (see diagram). This will form a division line so the two halves of the papier-mâché egg shape can be separated easily.

3. With the felt-tipped pen, draw a circle 1 inch in diameter around the neck of the balloon. Also draw a 2-inch circle at the center of the top half of the balloon (see diagram).

4. Mix flour and water paste, and cut newspaper into 1-inch strips. Read the directions at the beginning of this chapter for both processes. Also read the directions for applying the paste-moistened strips to the balloon.

5. Apply the strips of paste-moistened newspaper to the balloon. Bring the strips up to the edge of the heavy cord, but do not cover it. Also do not cover either the circle on top of the balloon or the circle around the neck of the balloon.

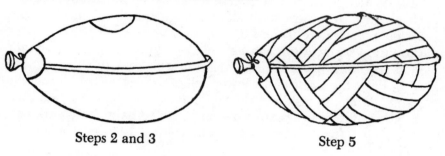

Steps 2 and 3   Step 5

6. Build up the papier-mâché until it is ¼ inch thick. Let dry.

7. When the papier-mâché is dry, gently pull the cord away from the balloon. Then, with the scissors, cut into the balloon all around this center line and around the edges of the two circles. If the balloon cannot be easily pulled away from the papier-mâché shell, do not worry; just trim the balloon along the edges. Add two layers of papier-mâché over the balloon on the inside of the two halves of the egg. Let dry.

8. Cut a 1-inch strip of cardboard, long enough to fit around the opening of the lower half of the egg. Glue ½ inch around the inside edge of the egg, leaving ½ inch above the opening (see diagram). Hold in place with a strip of masking tape if necessary. This collar will keep the top half of the egg from slipping when the two halves are glued together.

9. Put two or three strips of paste-moistened paper together. Twist them into a rope; dip into paste, and attach to the center

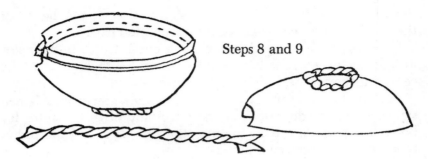

Steps 8 and 9

bottom of the egg in an oval shape (see diagram). Let dry. Make the same rope edging around the cut-out circle on the top half of the egg.

10. When the bottom rope support and the rope around the circle are dry, turn the lower half of the egg upright. Sandpaper the inside of each half of the egg, and dust with a soft brush. Cover the inside surfaces of each half of the egg with acrylic polymer gloss medium, using the flat nylon brush. Let dry.

11. Paint the inside of the lower half of the egg with white acrylic paint. Paint the inside of the top half of the egg with pale blue acrylic paint, using the flat nylon brush to paint both surfaces. (See page 6 for directions on mixing colors.) Let dry, then add a second coat, and let dry.

12. Form a scene inside the lower half of the egg with paste-soaked newspaper strips: mountains, a lake, fields, a small square house, or whatever you like. Let dry.

Step 12

13. Smooth any rough areas with sandpaper. Brush away dust or paper crumbles with a dry brush. Cover all surfaces with acrylic polymer gloss medium, using the #4 brush. Let dry. Then paint the scene with different shades of green; a blue lake; white house with a red roof; light green, yellow, and dirt-brown fields, using both the #2 and #4 brushes. Let dry, then add a second coat if necessary, and let it dry.

14. Brush thinned-out white glue over the outside upper half of the cardboard collar and over the edges of both halves of the egg. Put the top half over the bottom half, and let the glue dry.

15. Cover the joining crack with newspaper strips soaked with paste, first centered over the crack, then criss-crossed over this first layer and spreading out over the egg. Let dry a bit. Add a rope of soaked newspaper strips around this joining area, and also around the edge of the front round opening, following directions in Step 9. Let dry.

16. Sandpaper the outside of the egg and dust off with a dry brush. Cover the entire surface with acrylic polymer gloss medium, using the flat brush. Let dry. Cover egg with acrylic paint in white, light tan, or any light color of your choice, again using the flat brush. Let dry, and add a second coat if necessary, letting it dry before the next step. Paint all the rope areas a contrasting color, or white if the egg is a color. Let dry, and add a second coat if necesary. Let dry.

17. Now peek through the front opening, and you will see the scene spread out before you, lighted from the top opening.

Variation: You can make an egg with a large top opening and no front opening. Then view the scene from above.

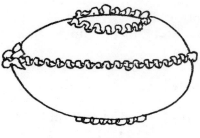

Variation

TUMBLE TOY

Make a Humpty-Dumpty or clown tumble toy of newspaper papier-mâché strips over a balloon base. Decorate the surface with acrylic paints. Weight the bottom with sand or gravel glued in place. Then your toy can be pushed over but will always roll back to an upright position.

Materials and Tools
2 balloons, 4 inches and 2 inches (unblown length)
white household glue
newspapers
flour and water paste
thin string
sand or small size bird gravel, 4 to 5 tablespoons
typewriter paper
acrylic polymer gloss medium
tubes of acrylic paint: white, black, red, yellow,
    and blue

pencil
ruler
scissors
black felt-tipped pen
tablespoon
flat nylon brush, 1 inch wide
round nylon brushes, #2 and #4
small containers for mixing paint

Directions

1. Blow up the two balloons; twist the ends, then tie each neck with string. Brace the balloons upright between jars and fill the necks with white glue; let dry. This will seal the opening and there will be no loss of air in the balloon while you are working. Make the larger balloon about 6 inches in diameter and the smaller one 2¾ inches in diameter—or you can choose your own sizes.

2. With the felt-tipped pen, mark a 1½-inch circle around the neck of the larger balloon.

3. Cut 1-inch wide strips of newspaper to be used in covering the balloons. Mix flour and water paste. See directions at the beginning of this chapter for preparing and applying newspaper-strip papier-mâché.

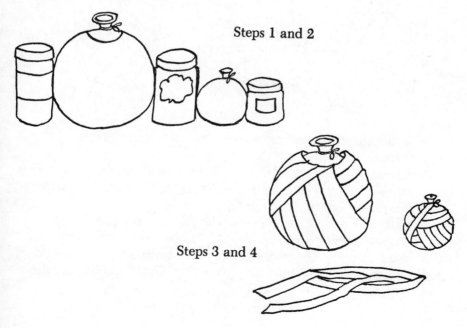

Steps 1 and 2

Steps 3 and 4

4. Apply the paste-soaked newspaper strips to the larger balloon, leaving the marked circle around the neck uncovered. Set the covered balloon aside to dry. Then cover the smaller balloon with papier-mâché, leaving only the neck itself uncovered. Set aside to dry. The papier-mâché is ⅜ inch thick on both balloons,

5. When the two papier-mâché covered balloons are dry, cut away the exposed circle on the larger balloon. Leave the rest of the balloon inside if stuck; otherwise pull it out. Brace the papier-mâché form with the open circle at the top. Pour 2 to 3 tablespoons of white glue into the inside bottom of the balloon. Sprinkle 4 to 5 tablespoons of sand or fine gravel over the glue, and mix in lightly. *Do not disturb until glue is thoroughly dry.*

6. Place the small balloon on top of the large balloon with its neck down into the hole of the large balloon. Add a line of white glue around the edge of the hole to hold the smaller balloon in place. Let dry. Then add two or three criss-crossing layers of papier-mâché strips over the joint, spreading them out over the surfaces of the two balloons. Let dry.

Step 5

Step 6

7. Sandpaper the surface to remove any rough edges of the paper strips.

8. Cover all surfaces of the tumble toy with acrylic polymer gloss medium, using the flat 1-inch wide brush. Let dry. Add a second coat if needed, and let dry.

9. Paint the tumbletoy with acrylic paint, using the flat brush for the larger surfaces and the #2 and #4 brushes for smaller areas and details. Follow the suggested designs, or make your own design (see page 6 for directions on mixing and applying acrylic paint).

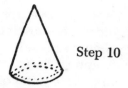

Step 10

10. If you are making a clown, add a cone-shaped hat made from typewriter paper. You can cover the hat with two or three layers of papier-mâché strips of newspaper. When dry, finish with acrylic polymer gloss medium and then with acrylic paint. Glue a strip of heavy cord around the inside bottom of the hat. When dry, glue the hat to the clown's head.

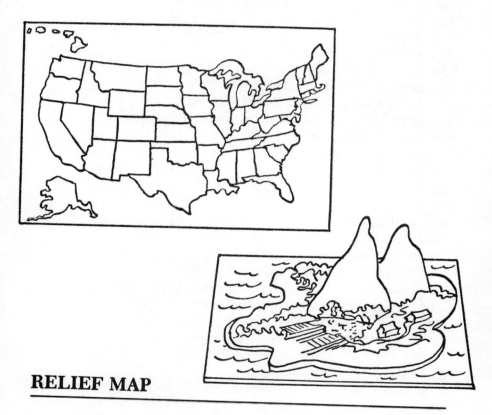

RELIEF MAP

Make a relief map with instant papier-mâché pulp. It can be whatever you choose: a United States map; your own state, village, town, or city; your own neighborhood; a summer camp; or an imagined place or one from a story—perhaps a treasure island. The map is painted with acrylic or poster paints: green and earth brown for the land; pale yellow for sand; blue for lakes and oceans; and gray for highways and city areas. Check an atlas for a contour map of mountain and plains areas of the United States or your own state. Mount your map on a sheet of heavy cardboard.

Materials and Tools
instant papier-mâché, 16-ounce package
tracing paper or onionskin typewriter paper,
    size of map you are copying
white drawing paper, size of your finished map
thin cardboard (optional)
wax paper
heavy cardboard (base for map)
clear self-sticking tape
acrylic polymer gloss medium
tubes of acrylic paint, your choice of colors
jars of poster paint, your choice of colors (optional)
white household glue
black felt-tipped pen
pencil
ruler
scissors
craft knife
tools for mixing instant papier-mâché
    (see manufacturer's directions)
flat nylon brush, 1 inch wide (for acrylic paint)
flat watercolor brush, 1 inch wide (for poster paint)
round nylon brushes, #2 and #4 (for acrylic paint)
round watercolor brushes, #2 and #4 (for poster paint)
small containers for mixing paint

Directions
    1. If you are following an exact map of a country or state, make a grid on a sheet of tracing or onionskin paper (the same size as the map you are copying). Measure and cut a sheet of heavy white drawing paper or light cardboard the size of your finished map. Make an enlarged grid on this sheet.

2. Place the tracing paper grid over the map to be copied. Do not trace the map, just look through the tracing paper at the map beneath it. Enlarge this map on the heavy paper grid using a pencil, then draw over the pencil lines with the black felt-tipped pen. See enlarging directions on page 4.

3. Put a sheet of tracing paper over the drawing paper map and trace this enlarged map with the felt-tipped pen. If your sheets of paper are too small, put enough sheets together with self-sticking tape. Set the traced map aside to use as a guide when filling in the details on the papier-mâché map.

4. Place a sheet of wax paper (at least 3 inches wider all around) over the drawing paper map. (You can make a large sheet by attaching separate widths of wax paper with clear self-sticking tape.) Hold the edges down on the working surface with self-sticking tape.

5. Following the manufacturer's directions carefully, mix the instant papier-mâché.

6. Build up the map on the wax paper surface, covering the whole area of the map with a ⅜-inch thick layer of instant papier-mâché. Now start to contour the map, adding mountains, valleys, plains, rivers, lakes, roads, and cities—all in relief. If your map is an island or a coastal area, add the ocean area. Let the papier-mâché dry until hard.

7. When the map is dry, cover all surfaces with acrylic polymer gloss medium, using the flat, 1-inch wide nylon brush. Let dry, then add another coat if needed, and let dry. Turn the map over very carefully and cover the back with the acrylic polymer gloss medium (first remove the wax paper). Use only one coat.

8. Paint the right side of the map with the colors of your choice, using either acrylic paint or poster paint. Add a second coat if needed, after letting the first coat dry. Use the flat nylon brush for large areas of acrylic paint, and the flat watercolor brush for poster paint. The #2 and #4 round brushes are for smaller areas and details; nylon for acrylic paint, watercolor brushes for poster paint.

9. Cut a piece of cardboard a little larger than your map (if the map is irregular in shape, like a state or a country), using the craft knife and ruler. Cut the cardboard to the same size if you have edged your island with water in a square or rectangular shape. With an irregular map, paint the area of the cardboard outside the map's edges first with acrylic polymer gloss medium; let it dry, then paint it with a background color of your choice. Let this dry, and add a second coat of color if necessary. Do not paint the cardboard if the map area is a square or rectangle.

10. Spread thinned-out white glue over the center area of the cardboard, following the outline of the irregularly shaped map. Lift the map very carefully and place it over the glue. Let dry. If the map is the same shape as the cardboard, cover the whole unpainted surface of the cardboard with white glue. If the glue soaks in too much, add a second coat. Place the map over the glue, and let dry.

Suggestion: If you are planning high mountains on your imaginary map, make cones from typewriter paper, and put them in position on your map. Cover the cones with instant papier-mâché. Drying will be easier, as only a thin coating of papier-mâché will have to dry, instead of a thick wad of material.

HAND-PUPPET HEAD

Hand puppets are fun to make and play with. The basic head shape is easily formed of papier-mâché over a small balloon. The features are pinched and molded in the wet papier-mâché. When dry, paint the face and hair with acrylic paint. Mold the hands from papier-mâché and paint them. The dress is a simple covering for your hand made from cloth or rice paper.

Materials and Tools
small rubber balloon
sewing thread
white household glue
newspaper
flour and water paste
thin cardboard, 1 × 2¾ inches
paper clips
white self-sticking tape or masking tape, 1 inch wide
sandpaper
tubes of acrylic paint: white, black, and red
    (blue, yellow, and brown optional)
typewriter paper
small piece of cloth or fibrous rice paper
pencil
ruler
scissors
thin nail
felt-tipped pen
round nylon brushes, #2 and #4
small containers for mixing paint and paste
needle and thread

Directions

1. Blow up the balloon until it is 2 to 2½ inches in diameter. Tie the neck of the balloon with string or thread, and cut off extra string. Prop up the balloon so the neck is facing upward. Fill the cup of the neck end with white glue and let it dry until stiff. This will keep the air from leaking out of the balloon while you are covering it with papier-mâché.

2. With the felt-tipped pen, draw a circle ¾ inch in diameter around the base of the balloon's neck.

3. Prepare newspaper strips and flour and water paste, following the directions at the beginning of this chapter.

4. When the glue in the neck of the balloon is dry, cover the balloon with strips of paste-soaked newspaper. Do not cover the circular area drawn around the neck.

5. Build up the papier-mâché to almost ¼ inch thick around the balloon. Turn the balloon upside down and brace it in a

water glass, taping to hold it steady. Now, with the thin nail and your fingers, plus torn-up bits of paste-soaked paper, mold the features of the face—eyebrows, eyes, nose, mouth, chin, ears, and hair. Let head dry.

6. When the papier-mâché is dry, cut away the ¾-inch circle of balloon plus neck. If the balloon is loose inside the head, remove it. Edge the round opening with tape, half inside and half outside the cut edge.

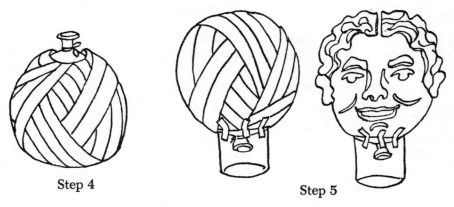

Step 4   Step 5

7. Curve a 1 × 2¾-inch strip of lightweight cardboard into a tube, ¾ inch in diameter with a ¼-inch overlap. Glue the ends together and hold them with a paper clip until dry. When dry, make cuts all around one end, ¼ inch apart and ¼ inch deep; bend the cut pieces of paper outward. Put glue on the underside of these pieces and slip the tube into the opening in the head, cut pieces inside. Slip your finger inside and press the cut edge down all around the inside of the head. Let dry.

Step 7

8. Tape the outside of the tube to the head, applying half the width of the tape to the tube and half to the head.

9. Cover tube and tape with three or four layers of papier-mâché strips, blending them up onto the head. Let dry.

10. Cut out hands from lightweight cardboard. Cover with several layers of papier-mâché. Let dry.

Step 10

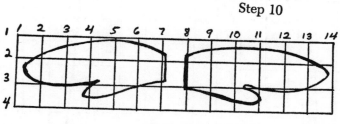

Enlarge to ¼ " squares

11. Sandpaper head and hands so the surfaces are smooth. Paint the head, neck, and hands with acrylic polymer gloss medium, using the #4 brush. Let dry. To color the face, neck, and hands, mix a little of the red with the white paint, and apply with the #4 brush. Add a second coat if needed after the first coat has dried. Let the second coat dry. Put a little more red in the skin color and add it to the cheeks; use the #2 brush to add red for the lips, black for the eyebrows, eyes, and hair. Let dry. You can cover the head, neck, and hands with a final coat of acrylic polymer gloss medium.

12. Enlarge the pattern of the dress by the grid method on the sheet of typewriter paper. Lay the pattern over the cloth or rice paper and cut out. Sew or glue arm and side seams together on the wrong side. Turn back to the right side, and turn under the edges of the sleeves. Put a hand into one sleeve opening at the top edge, and hold in position with white glue. Glue the edges of the sleeve opening together. Repeat with the other sleeve. Put a book over both sleeves until the glue is dry. Add dress details with acrylic paint.

13. Slip the dress neck over the papier-mâché neck. Turn under a narrow seam all around the neck, and glue the seam to the neck. Let the glue dry.

14. Put your middle finger into the head and your thumb and little finger into the arms to move head and arms. The dress will cover your hand.

Fold   Fold

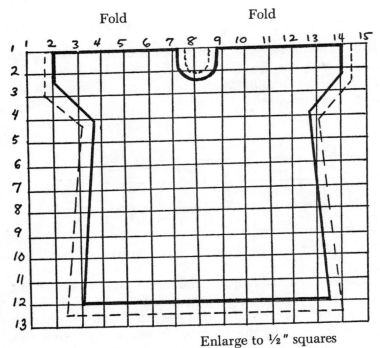

Enlarge to ½" squares

Step 12

Step 13

Variations: You can make a larger head. Or you can make several heads: Punch and Judy, or a princess and prince and a wicked witch.

If you are using instant papier-mâché for other projects, you can use it for the head and hands of the puppet, following directions at the beginning of the chapter.

Making and
Decorating Boxes

The projects in this chapter can be made with boxes you'll find around the house, gift boxes you have bought, or cardboard cartons from the grocery store. If you cannot find the right size box, follow the directions for making a box to your own measurements.

Techniques of Making a Box and Cover

First, decide on the measurements of your box—width, length, and depth. Next, choose the material for the box—lightweight or corrugated cardboard, bristol board, poster board, or illustration board. With ruler and pencil, measure the width and length of the bottom of the box in the center of the board. The pencil lines are made on the right side of the board. Measure and outline the four sides, adding ¼- to 1-inch wide flaps on two opposite sides (see diagram).

Cut around the outline of the box with scissors or a craft knife braced against a ruler. Score the lines around the bottom of the

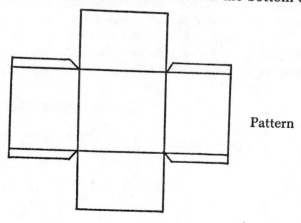

Pattern

box and the four flaps (see page 42). Bend the four sides into an upright position. Bend the flaps at right angles to the sides.

Cover the flaps with white glue and press them against the other two sides of the box. Slip a large paper clip over the top edge of each flap to hold it in place while the glue is drying. If the box is a very deep one, run a strip of masking tape along the length of the flap on the inside, half on the flap and half on the box side.

The box cover is made as a shallow box. The measurements of the top of the cover are based on the *outside* measurements of the box, plus ⅟₁₆ inch extra all around the edges, so the cover can be slipped off easily. Then follow the instructions for making a box.

Gluing the box

Corner

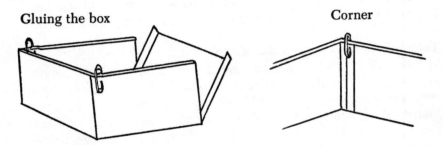

Covering a Box With Paper

To cover a box with decorative paper, measure and cut the paper as if you were making a box.

Measure the *outside* of the box for the outside covering; measure the *inside* of the box for the inside lining. The very slight difference in the measurements allows for the thickness of the board. The only additional measurement is an extra ½-inch flap around the top of the outside covering. This flap is turned over and glued to the inside of the box, covering the top edge of the board. Repeat for the box cover.

Covering the box

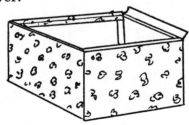

RECIPE FILE BOX

This open-top file box can be used for recipes, addresses, or any other set of cards that have to be kept in one place. The size of the box is based on the ordinary file card size, 3 × 5 inches. If you are using larger cards, then change the measurements of the box.

The box is made of white illustration board or colored poster board. The white illustration board is covered with Con-Tact paper. Add decorations cut from a food magazine, or other decorations to fit the contents of the box.

Materials and Tools
illustration board or stiff colored poster board
file cards
bristol board (see Step 4)
Con-Tact paper, your choice of color
decorations cut from magazines or other
    printed papers
white household glue
white masking tape, ½ inch wide
pencil
ruler
scissors
4 large paper clips
flat watercolor brush, 1 inch wide
small container for mixing glue

Directions

1. To make the box, follow the directions at the beginning of this chapter. The bottom of the box is 3 × 5½ inches; the sides are 3½ inches high.

2. If you are using white illustration board, cover the outside of the box with Con-Tact paper in your choice of color. Either buy paper or use paper left over from another project. On the back of the sheet, measure and draw with pencil and ruler the measurements of the outside of the box. Cut it out with the scissors. Apply it to the box, following the manufacturer's directions. See the diagram at the beginning of the chapter.

3. Cut out food designs from magazines or small pictures from gift wrap paper, postcards, or any other printed papers. Thin the white glue with a little water and brush it lightly over the back of each picture. Put it in position on the box and pat down with a wad of facial tissue.

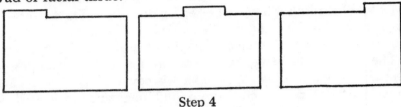

Step 4

4. Cut out twelve cards from the lightweight bristol board. These are the same size as the file cards, *plus* a ½ by 1 inch tab at the top. On four of the cards the tab is at the left-hand edge; on four of the cards it is in the middle; on four of the cards it is at the right-hand edge. The tabs are used to identify the contents of the file cards behind each tabbed card. If this is to be an address file, then make 26 cards, one for each letter of the alphabet; make eight cards with each tab position, plus two extra cards for the middle position.

TRINKET BOX

The basic box with a lid can be bought at the dime store, or you can make your own, following directions at the beginning of this

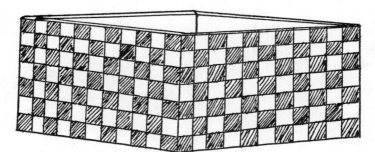

chapter. The decoration is made of small squares of Con-Tact paper in two alternating colors—black and silver, silver and red, red and black, or any combination you like. This is also a way to use up Con-Tact paper left over from other projects.

Materials and Tools
box with lid, 5½ × 5½ × 3½ inches
Con-Tact paper, any two colors
materials for making a box (optional)
pencil
ruler
scissors

Directions
   1. Measure, vertically and horizontally, the front and one side of the box. Divide the measurements into even squares or rectangles for the pieces to be cut from Con-Tact paper. The pieces should be no larger than ½ to ⅝ inch.
   2. For the best design, the number of pieces, vertically and horizontally, should be an uneven number. For instance, box measurements of 5½ × 5½ × 3½ will work out to 11 pieces ½ inch square along the horizontal rows on each side; 7 pieces ½ inch square along the vertical rows; the cover rows will contain 11 squares both ways (see diagram). You will have to work out a special size for the pieces for the sides of the lid—either two rows or one row of pieces.
   Using an odd number of rows means that top and bottom rows will match; the corners will have a pattern of two squares of matching colors to set them off from the sides of the box (see

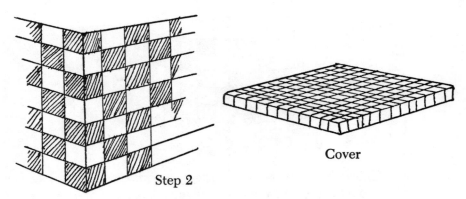

Step 2

Cover

diagram). So check the measurements of a box before you buy it, or make a box to the right size. Boxes can be rectangular rather than square.

3. Once you decide on the final size of the pieces, measure and draw vertical and horizontal lines on the sides and cover of the box to the same measurement as the pieces. These lines will be your guide in placing the alternate color pieces in position.

4. On the back of the two sheets of Con-Tact paper, measure and draw the lines for the pieces. Half of the pieces will be cut from one color, the rest will be cut from the other color. Cut out the pieces with the scissors and put them in two separate piles.

5. Apply the pieces to the box sides, peeling off the backing of each piece as you are ready to use it. Start at the top row of one side with the darker color at the corner, and alternate the colors. The next row will start with the lighter color, and so down the line, alternating colors.

6. If you have made a box of plain, unfinished cardboard, or if the illustration board has a tan back with printing on it, line the inside of the box and cover with solid-color Con-Tact.

MEMO PAD AND WRITING PAPER HOLDERS

This is really like making a box with only three sides instead of five sides. The basic materials are illustration board, self-sticking fabric or plastic tape, printed paper, and a memo pad and pen. The pad can be any size from a small 3 × 5½ inches all the way

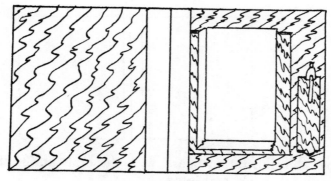

Memo Pad Holder

up to a legal-size yellow pad. As soon as a pad is used up, another one can be inserted in the holder. Then you'll always have a handy pad at the telephone or on a desk. These make neat gifts for relatives and friends.

Materials and Tools
memo pad, your choice of size
illustration board or cardboard
bristol board or lightweight cardboard
printed paper: wallpaper, gift wrap, shelf paper,
    or your own paper
ballpoint pen
self-sticking fabric or plastic tape,
    1 to 1½ inches wide
white household glue
pencil
ruler
scissors
craft knife
soft watercolor brush, 1 inch wide
small container for mixing glue

Directions for Memo Pad Holder
1. The front and back covers for the memo pad are 1¼ inches wider on all sides than the pad. The center strip called a "spine" is ¼ inch wider than the thickness of the pad and pen. Measure

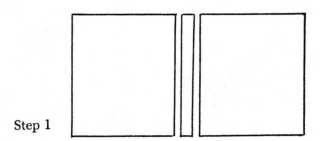

Step 1

and cut the illustration board with the craft knife into three pieces—front, back, and spine.

2. Cover the outside of the front and back pieces of illustration board with printed paper. The outside covering paper is ½ inch wider on all four sides. This margin is turned over and glued down to the inside of the cardboard. The inside covering paper is the same size as the board and so covers the turned-down margin. Follow instructions for gluing in the Cut and Glue chapter. Let the glued pieces dry under a weight.

3. While the paper is drying, measure and cut the bristol board or lightweight cardboard 1¼ inch narrower than the width of the back board, and 2 inches less than the length of the back board (see diagram). Cover both sides with printed paper, following directions in Step 2. Let dry under a weight.

4. Attach the covered bristol board to the back board with white glue brushed along a ½-inch margin on the two sides and bottom (see diagram). Put a weight on the board until the glue is dry.

5. Cut a length of tape ½ inch longer than the covered boards. Lay it flat on the working surface, sticky side up. Put the center spine over the tape so that the tape covers one-half the width of the spine, and ¼ inch of tape is left exposed top and bottom. Press down on the board. Next, place the front board in position over the tape, ⅛ inch away from the spine board, and with ¼ inch of tape left exposed top and bottom. Press down on the board. Bring the ¼-inch pieces of tape—top and bottom—over the edges of the two boards. Repeat the taping of the other half of the spine and the back board.

6. Cut a length of tape, the exact length of the boards, and

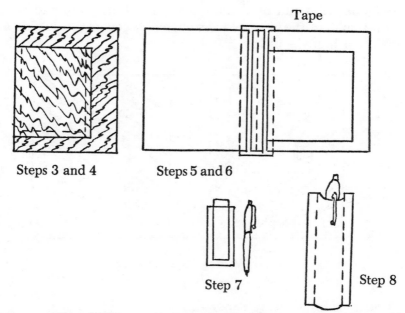

Steps 3 and 4   Steps 5 and 6

Tape

Step 7   Step 8

place over the *inside* area of the board and spine in the same position as the outside tape. Press tape firmly against the ⅛ inch exposed sticky surface of tape. Repeat on the back board and the other half of the spine (see diagram).

7. Finally, make the pen holder and attach it to the back board beside the memo pad pocket. Cut two 5-inch pieces of tape. Trim away ½ inch from one long side and one end of one piece of tape. Center this narrower piece on the broader one, sticky sides together. Cut two small squares from the corners of one narrow end, and turn over the center piece (see diagram).

8. Put the tape pen holder in position on the right side of the back board beside the pad pocket, pressing down the left edge *only*. Slip the pen into position between the board and the tape before pressing down on the other side and the lower edge of the tape. You may want to add a ½-inch width of tape around the three sides of the holder, half on the holder and the other half on the back board.

9. Slip the cardboard backing of the pad into the top of the bristol board pocket to hold the memo pad in place. Slip the pen clip over the top of its tape pocket, and your project is complete.

Variation: You can bind the top edge of the memo pad pocket with a strip of the tape folded so one half covers the outside and the other half the inside.

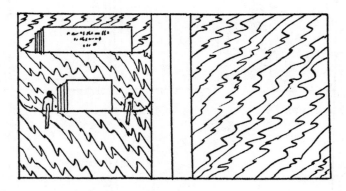

Writing Paper Holder

Directions for Writing Paper Holder

1. This has to be made large enough to hold writing paper and envelopes in two separate pockets, so the size of the basic illustration boards and the bristol board pockets depends on the writing paper and envelope size, plus a pen.

2. Follow Steps 1 and 2 for the basic cutting and covering of the boards. Make and cover two bristol board pockets and attach them to the *front* cover. These are the full width of the front cover (see diagram for proportions and placement). Follow Steps 5 and 6 for putting holder together.

3. You can decorate the front of the holder with a label and decoupage cut-outs.

DOLL CHAIR

Doll chairs are easily made from any tube-shaped cardboard container. One half of the tube is cut away lengthwise to form a straight or wing-shaped chair back. The cover, tucked into the round opening of the tube, becomes the seat. The whole is covered with small-patterned or striped paper.

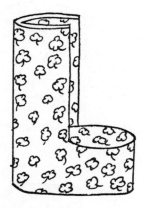 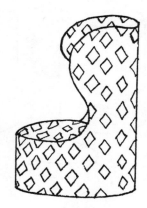

Materials and Tools
tube-shaped cardboard carton, your choice of size
patterned paper
white household glue
pencil
ruler
scissors
craft knife
flat watercolor brush, 1 inch wide
small dish for mixing glue

Directions

1. Pick a carton, depending on the size of the doll. An oatmeal box, 7 × 4 inches, is one choice. Remove the top cover of the box and dust out the interior. From the bottom of the box, measure one-quarter of the depth of the box. At this point, draw a pencil line halfway around the circumference of the box. From each end of this line draw a straight line to the top of the box, or a double-curve line for a wing chair back (see drawing, page 146). Cut out along these lines with scissors or craft knife.

2. Cover the chair, outside and inside, with patterned paper. Glue patterned paper to the outside and edges of the cover. Let the glue dry.

3. Put a thin coat of glue around the outside edge of the cover and force the cover into the opening of the seat area. This will be a tight fit, which is good. The cover may curve upward a bit,

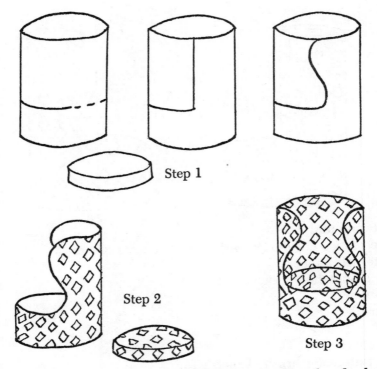

Step 1

Step 2

Step 3

making it look more like a cushioned seat. Let the glue dry before using the chair.

Variation: For dollhouse size chairs, use a length of mailing tube, paper towel, or bathroom paper tube. Make the seat from a circle of lightweight cardboard, adding an outside margin to be turned down. Score around the inner circle and slash the margin edge every ¼ inch (see diagram).

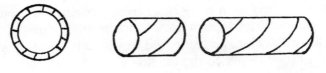

Variation

COMPARTMENTED TREASURE BOX

Everyone needs a flat, covered or uncovered box to hold small items. A desktop box holds paper clips, rubber bands, a roll of stamps, ballpoint pens and refills, pencils, rubber erasers, and many other small things. A workshop space needs storage for all sorts of small screws, nails, washers, fuses, and cotter pins. In the kitchen, small tools, cookie cutters, pastry tubes, and can openers, which all get lost in a large drawer, will have their own places. In a dresser drawer, a compartmented box can hold cuff links, tie clasps, earrings, pins, and necklaces. Compartmented boxes make good gifts; plan the size of the spaces to fit their use.

Materials and Tools
box, with or without a cover, 2 to 3 inches deep
illustration board: size depends on box to be made
    (see Step 4)
typewriter paper
masking tape
self-sticking tape
decorative paper or Con-Tact
white household glue
pencil
ruler
scissors
craft knife
flat watercolor brush, 1 inch wide
small dish for mixing glue

Directions
   1. Either buy or make a box of the size you need for your compartmented box. See directions in the beginning of this chapter for making a box and cover.
   2. If your box is to be larger than 8½ × 11 inches, put sheets of typewriter paper together with either self-sticking tape or masking tape to make a sheet the same size as the bottom of the box.
   3. Plan the number of compartments and their sizes on the

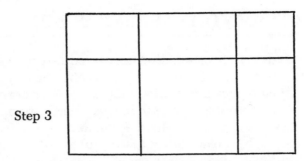

Step 3

sheet of paper, measuring and ruling the lines. When you are planning spaces for pens, pencils, or special small tools, be sure to make compartments the right length and width.

4. Once your design is made, measure the length of each separate dividing strip. All strips are the same depth as the box. Buy enough standard size illustration board to make all the strips.

5. Measure and cut the strips from the illustration board with a craft knife. To fit them together, cut each strip at the joining point. One strip is cut halfway up from the bottom; the other strip is cut halfway down from the top (see diagram). When these two slots are pushed together, they hold the strips securely, and the top and bottom will be even with the box depth. However, do not put the strips together until they are covered with the lining paper.

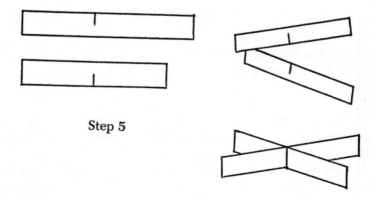

Step 5

6. Cover the outside of the box with patterned or plain paper. Line the inside of the box with matching or contrasting paper.

Follow the directions at the beginning of this chapter. Cover both sides of the strips with the lining paper. When dry, cut through to the slots in the board and put the strips together to form compartments.

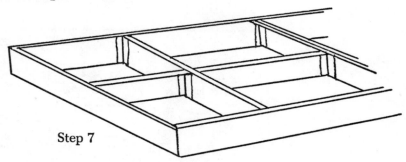

Step 7

7. Place the compartmented strips inside the box. Hold the ends in place against the sides with short, ½-inch wide strips of the lining paper. Fold the strips in half and glue into position, one-half on the divider, one-half on the side of the box (see diagram).

Variation: Use this same compartment method to fill a drawer with separating strips of covered illustration board or heavy cardboard, fitting them to the exact size of the drawer. Line the bottom of the drawer with paper, but do not glue it in place.

SHOW-OFF BOXES

Collect a number of small boxes of different sizes, shapes, and depths, with and without lids. If you cannot find five or six boxes and their lids, then make the boxes following the simple directions at the beginning of this chapter. The boxes are placed bottoms up—the lids tops up—on a solid color posterboard backing. They are held in place with self-sticking tape in the same or contrasting color as the poster board. Pictures are glued to the box bottoms—family pictures, travel pictures, your favorite art pictures—and the whole arrangement hung on a wall.

Materials and Tools
5 or 6 small boxes and lids, round,
    square and rectangular, 4 to 7 inches
colored poster board, any color
self-sticking tape or masking tape,
    1½ to 2 inches wide
pictures, sizes to fit the boxes
white household glue
cord
wall hook
pencil
ruler
scissors

craft knife
nail
materials and tools for making boxes (optional)
flat watercolor brush, 1 inch wide
container for mixing glue

Directions

1. Assemble the small boxes on your working surface. Five or six boxes with lids will give you a choice of ten to twelve holders for pictures. Choose boxes approximately the same sizes as the pictures you want to use. If the pictures are a bit smaller, cover the exposed cardboard edges with tape. For best results, the boxes should not be over 1½ inches deep.

2. If you want to make boxes to fit your pictures, follow directions in the beginning of this chapter. Boxes can be different depths, from ½ to 1½ inches.

3. Attach the pictures to the flat, outside surface of the boxes with thinned-out white glue. Let them dry before starting Step 4.

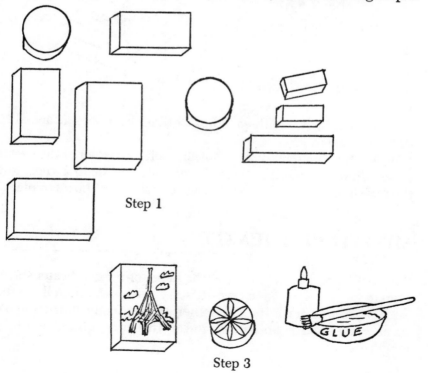

Step 1

Step 3

4. Arrange the boxes on a flat working surface until the arrangement pleases you. See the drawing for suggestions. Measure the arrangement; then measure and cut the poster board with the craft knife braced against the ruler, allowing a 2- to 3-inch margin all around.

5. Place boxes in position on the poster board. Mark their positions with pencil dots at each corner.

6. Starting with the upper left-hand box, cover the sides with tape. Allow a ½-inch tape overhang all around the open bottom edge. Make a cut at each corner of the ½-inch margin. Pull the margin tape outward, and place the corners of the box on the matching pencil dots on the poster board. Press tape smoothly over the board to hold the box in position. Trim away any extra tape that extends above the top of the box, unless you need it to cover the space between the edge of a picture and the box side.

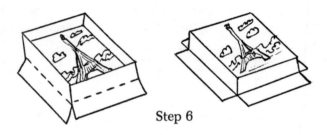

Step 6

7. Repeat Step 6 with each box until all boxes are attached to the poster board.

8. With a thin nail, make a hole in each top corner of the poster board. Push a cord end through each hole and tie in a knot. Put the wall hook in position, and hang your show-off boxes in place.

MINIATURE THEATER

Start with a cardboard carton as the basic form for a theater stage. Plan to use a scene from a favorite story, such as Cinderella in the kitchen, just as her fairy godmother arrives. You can then make scenery and characters for the rest of the story, and give a full-length show.

Materials and Tools
cardboard carton, any size
bristol board, dull surface
typewriter paper
lead pencil transfer paper
white household glue
7 round wood dowels, ⅜ inch in diameter (see Step 6)
masking tape, ¾ inch wide
tubes of acrylic paint or jars of poster paint:
    white, black, brown, red, and yellow
acrylic polymer gloss medium
Con-Tact paper, wood-grained (optional)
pencil
ruler
scissors
craft knife
craft saw
flat watercolor brush, 1 inch wide
flat nylon brush, 1 inch wide
round nylon brushes, #2, #4, and #5
small containers for mixing glue and paints

Directions
   1. With scissors or craft knife, remove the loose flaps on top of the box. Also remove the two short flaps on the inside bottom of the box, leaving attached the two long flaps which will hold the stage floor.
   2. Use the grid method to enlarge the pattern for the front of the stage on two sheets of typewriter paper held together by mask-

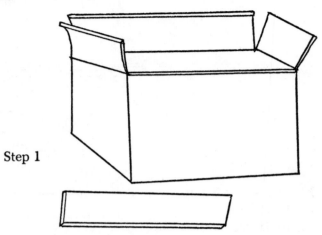

Step 1

ing tape. Proportion the pattern to fit whatever size box you are using. Cut out the paper pattern. Hold it against one long side of the box and trace around the edges. The area above the dotted line is held above the top edge of the box. Cut away the outlined center area of the box with scissors and craft knife (see diagrams).

3. On the sheet of bristol board, first lay down the lead pencil

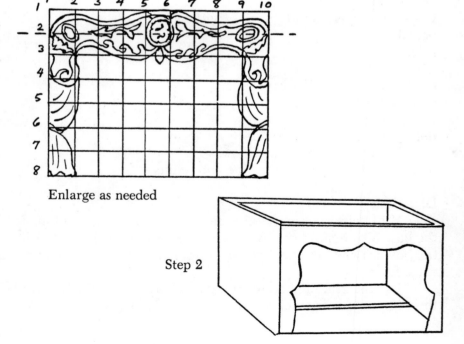

Enlarge as needed

Step 2

transfer paper, then the paper pattern. Trace around the edges of the pattern, and fill in the details of curtain and top decoration. Remove pattern and transfer paper, and cut out the bristol board front with scissors and craft knife.

4. Thin the white glue with water. With the inch-wide brush, put a light coat of glue on the back of the bristol board design, *except* the area above the dotted line. Also brush a light coat of glue over the box front. Put the bristol board design in position over the front of the box. Turn the box over so the bristol board is flat against the working surface. Place books over the glued area on the inside edge. Let the glue dry.

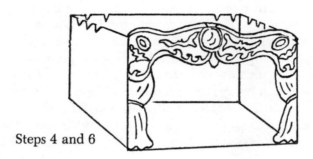

Steps 4 and 6

5. Measure the stage floor area, and cut a piece of bristol board to fit it. Glue the bristol board in position and place books on top until the glue dries. This will be painted or covered with wood-grained Con-Tact paper. Other floor coverings can be put temporarily in place.

6. The back and side wall scenery is made of bristol board hung by masking tape from dowels. The dowels are cut 4 to 6 inches longer than the width and length of the box. To support the dowels, make three slots ½ inch wide and ¾ inch deep at the top of each side wall, starting 1 inch away from the back of the box, spacing them according to the needed depth of the stage. Scenery hung on dowels can be placed in any one of the slots. Changing scenery is very easy—just lift the dowels and bristol board up and out of the box.

7. The dowels for the side walls will rest on the top edges of the front and back of the box. Glue a 1-inch strip of cardboard along the top edge of the front wall, cutting this strip from one of the discarded cardboard flaps. Cut slots ½ inch wide and ½ inch deep at the top of the front and back wall. Starting 1½ inches from each side of the carton, add the second set of slots toward the center, depending on the width of the stage area needed for a scene.

8. Cut bristol board for the back wall scenery 1 inch narrower than the width of the box and 1 inch shorter than the height of the box. Center the bristol board on the length of a dowel, ½ inch away from the dowel. Hold the bristol board in place with 3½-inch lengths of masking tape looped over the dowel every 2 or 3 inches and pressed against the front and back of the bristol board. Repeat with two more dowels for other sets of scenery.

9. Cut two pieces of bristol board for the side walls; make them 1¼ inch less than the length of the side wall, and 1 inch shorter than the height of the box. Attach each piece to a dowel, the front edge ¼ inch away from the inside front of the box and the top edge 1 inch away from the dowel. Repeat with two more dowels for a second set of side walls. See Step 8 for directions. Be sure that the tape loops do not block the side wall slits. The back wall scenery is always hung first, then the side walls are put in place.

10. Paint separate bristol board walls and floor, as well as the front piece, with acrylic polymer gloss medium. Let dry; then paint the wall pieces and front following the designs shown or using your own designs. Paint the floor or cover it with Con-Tact paper in a woodgrain design. Both the floor and the front addi-

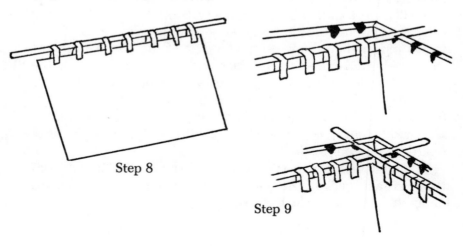

Step 8

Step 9

Step 10

tion should be level when painted, so turn box around for each step.

11. Make figures of the actresses and actors. Enlarge the figures of Cinderella and the fairy godmother by the grid method on typewriter paper, transferring them to the bristol board. Paint with acrylic paint. Add triangular supports so the two figures can stand upright on the stage (see diagram).

12. Now you can play the Cinderella scene in the kitchen. Use your imagination and make the coach scene, a ballroom scene, and other parts of the story. Or try another story, using these basic directions for making scenery and the actresses and actors.

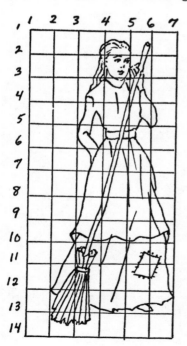

Enlarge as needed

Index